Standing Up
Standing Together

Property of

W. E. and Gilroy

April 7, '92

STANDING UP
STANDING TOGETHER

The Emergence of the
National Association of Evangelicals

ARTHUR H. MATTHEWS

Foreword by Billy Graham

National Association of Evangelicals
Carol Stream, Illinois
1992

STANDING UP, STANDING TOGETHER: THE EMERGENCE OF THE
NATIONAL ASSOCIATION OF EVANGELICALS

by Arthur H. Matthews

Copyright © 1992
National Association of Evangelicals
All Rights Reserved

Edited and designed by Dave and Neta Jackson
Cover design by Joe Ragont Studios
Printed in the United States of America

Published by the National Association of Evangelicals
450 Gundersen Dr.
Carol Stream, IL 60188
(708) 665-0500

NAE Office of Public Affairs
1023 Fifteenth Street NW, Suite 500
Washington, D.C. 20005
(202) 789-1011

The National Association of Evangelicals (NAE) is a coordinating agency facilitating Christian unity, public witness, and cooperative ministry among evangelical denominations, congregations, educational institutions, and related service organizations in the United States.

Library of Congress Cataloging-in-Publication Data

Matthews, Arthur H. (Arthur Hugh), 1933—
    Standing up, standing together : the emergence of the National Association of Evangelicals / Arthur H. Matthews ; foreword by Billy Graham.
    p.   cm.
    Includes biographical references and index.
    ISBN   1-880844-00-1 (pbk.)
    1. National Association of Evangelicals—History. 2. Evangelicalism—United States—History—20th century. 3. United States—Church History—20th century.   I. Title
BX6.N16M38   1992
280'.4'06073—dc20   91-43163
                                                                         CIP

In loving memory of three mentors
who taught—in word and deed—
what it means to be an evangelical:
L. Nelson Bell, Henry B. Dendy,
and G. Aiken Taylor.

Contents

Foreword

THE STUDY OF HISTORY has a way of putting things into perspective. Both people and institutions are shaped by influences and forces of which they are not always aware, but as time progresses, they more clearly understand life and its complexities. Therefore, a look at the emergence of the National Association of Evangelicals (NAE), as revealed in the following pages, has great value to American evangelicals, including myself, whose life and ministry parallel the history of NAE.

The book is written by a person well qualified for the task, Arthur H. Matthews. A seasoned and gifted journalist, Mr. Matthews has been a dispassionate observer of the evangelical scene for more than thirty years. An elder in the Presbyterian Church in America, he evidences a deep commitment to Jesus

Christ and his church. During his years of service to the Billy Graham Evangelistic Association, I found him to be a man of integrity and principle.

In tracing the history of NAE, *Standing Up, Standing Together* captures the moving story of the rise of a national coordinating agency for evangelicals at a time when few were predicting an evangelical resurgence in America. True to the principle that history is best written from a distance, Mr. Matthews spends most of his time on the early years. His focus is clearly personal, not institutional. Rather than simply chronicling events and activities as they happen, the writer probes the people behind the news, giving the story a highly human touch. As such, the book paints helpful portraits of many individuals, with their strengths and weaknesses, who made NAE what it is.

The book brought back many fond memories. I was graduated from Wheaton College and installed as pastor of the Village Church in suburban Western Springs just two months after NAE held its constitutional convention in Chicago in 1943. I first heard about NAE when J. Elwin Wright visited me. He, Harold J. Ockenga, Clyde W. Taylor, and Stephen W. Paine were all personal friends. In addition, I was fortunate enough to be well connected to the entire NAE network, which played a large role in the effectiveness of my early crusades. As I read the book, I was keenly aware that God himself was working behind NAE to help bring about a rediscovery of the gospel in America.

The book should serve well the National Association of Evangelicals, now fifty years old, at an important stage in history. Like evangelicalism in general, NAE faces a different nation and a different world than five decades ago. Equally important, NAE faces a different church and a different evangelical community. As NAE seeks to serve Christ, his people, and his church for another fifty years, the perspective offered in these pages should help in responding to the challenge of the future with wisdom, insight, and, most important, a better sense of history.

NAE has served evangelicals with distinction, providing needed structure, visibility, and stability. It has not achieved everything it set out to do, but *Standing Up, Standing Together* should help NAE as it seeks to uphold the evangelical cause with even greater effectiveness until our Lord returns.

Billy Graham
Montreat, North Carolina
October 1991

Preface

YOU SHOULD BE A TOUR GUIDE," viewers of my amateur slide shows sometimes blurt out once the lights are turned on. I never have been quite sure whether those people were advising me to leave journalism for another occupation or were just startled into saying something that sounded complimentary when awakened by the lights—or by a jab from a neighbor's elbow.

Since that unsolicited advice was not backed with any capital to establish a tour business, I stuck with reporting. Meanwhile, I continued to visit sites of historical significance. And I kept on taking pictures of those places—particularly the ones with a story about Christians who put their faith on the line.

As the fiftieth anniversary of the National Association of Evangelicals approached, I was asked to do something that might be considered a combination of journalism and tour leadership. NAE wanted a book pointing to the highlights of its half-century journey. After accepting the assignment, I began to realize what hard choices a guide must make. The passengers on his or her bus have different levels of interest in the various parts of territory they will visit. Within the agreed time and budget, the organizer plans an itinerary that gives all travelers an overview of the area, a few of its distinctives, and enough glimpses at other attractions to encourage a return trip.

Of necessity, the following look at NAE attempts only to show the big picture. Fifty years of accomplishments on a broad front nationally and internationally cannot be reported in detail in a small book. This will not satisfy the curiosity of everyone who wants to follow all the rabbit trails leading off the main road. I have happily left it to the specialists and academics to write their dissertations on more particular aspects of NAE's history. Surely, there will follow biographies of leaders as well as volumes on theological development, on the association's impact on particular phases of church and state history, and on the activities of the entities spawned under the NAE umbrella. I will look forward to learning from them.

A. H. M.

Acknowledgments

THE ASSISTANCE, SUPPORT, and encouragement of many people helped make this book a reality. All of those who helped are not listed here, but all are appreciated.

For access to materials, I am indebted to archivists of the Assemblies of God at Springfield, Missouri, of the Presbyterian Church in America at St. Louis, Missouri, and of the Billy Graham Center at Wheaton, Illinois. In addition, special thanks are due to Michael R. Alford for his help in finding the papers of former NAE President Herbert Mekeel in Schenectady, New York, to F. C. Fowler III for making available the papers of former NAE President Frederick Curtis Fowler in Elk Park, North Carolina, and to the family of Clyde W. Taylor, who provided access to his personal papers.

Those who submitted to interviews or who provided documents made a great contribution. The many interesting details that came to me this way put the "big picture" into perspective—even if all the details didn't find their way into the book.

Present and past NAE staff members have cooperated graciously. I am particularly grateful to Billy A. Melvin, executive director, and Robert W. Patterson, his associate, for their support. The assignment to undertake the task came from Dr. Melvin and from John H. White, then president, as a part of their planning for the association's fiftieth anniversary. They were bold to choose a reporter who has had little involvement in NAE. While they helped to make some of this history, they should not be held responsible for this particular recounting of it. All of its shortcomings are mine.

Heartfelt appreciation is expressed for the patience and understanding of colleagues at God's World Publications, especially Executive Editor Joel Belz. They were faithful in "minding the store" while I was working on this project.

1

The Wright Idea

IT TOOK UNTIL 1976 for some Americans to discover evangelicals. For others, it was four more years and another presidential campaign before they realized that a significant number of their neighbors believed the Bible and wanted its values reflected in national life.

Evangelicals discovered America centuries earlier.

Even Christopher Columbus has his partisans among evangelical scholars, who claim that the pre-Reformation explorer came to the New World in 1492 as an earnest Christian determined to propagate the gospel (the evangel, or Good News of Jesus Christ). Others say the first evangelicals in the Western Hemisphere were the French Protestants who tried to establish missionary beachheads in 1562 near present-day Jacksonville, Florida, and Parris Island, South Carolina. There were no doubt evangelical believers in North Carolina's 1584 "lost colony" and among Virginia's 1607 Jamestown settlers. The Pilgrim Fathers approaching Plymouth, Massachusetts, in 1620 documented their faith in the immortal Mayflower Compact, laying the spiritual foundations of a new country.

Evangelical Foundations in the New World

Since those first groups touched American soil, evangelicals have been a force in American history. They started the first schools and colleges. They were among the earliest political leaders. They provided a primitive communication "network" between the colonies. They began key commercial enterprises. They were the pioneers.

Despotic rule prompted the colonists who knew their Bibles to search the Scriptures. They realized that their problems ran deeper than the whims of the king or his governors. There were the basic questions of God's view of the worth of human beings and the role of those who would govern under God. Raising these questions brought evangelicals to the forefront of the struggle for independence. Their beliefs were influential in the foundational documents of the new nation. Christian volunteers were prominent as foot soldiers and commanders in the American Revolution.

Their contributions to the making of America were enormous, but the theological convictions of the contributors are often minimized or ignored by historians. Evangelical doctrine was, for generations, the doctrine of the major denominations. The country lived by a "biblical consensus" whether all of its citizens admitted it or not. Individual evangelicals saw little need to point out differences between themselves and their neighbors since, in all likelihood, the neighbors were also evangelicals. Evangelicals began to be taken for granted.

The Complacent Majority

As the nation grew, the religious picture changed. While Bible believers continued to play major personal roles, they had little to connect them or to represent them on the national scene. It was not so for the other groups. Roman Catholic and other newer faith groups were careful to maintain tight organizations which were vigilant against any threats—real or perceived—against their positions. Considerable attention was paid to putting qualified representatives of these faiths into key places at all levels of government and the media to see that their interests were represented.

From the early days of the United States, evangelicals associated themselves with each other across denominational lines in voluntary societies. Such bodies, however, were generally limited in scope. Each had a particular function, such as Bible distribution, maintenance of orphanages or other diaconal ministries, or evangelistic outreach to a specific sector of the population. These independent associations, such as the American Bible Society, did valuable pioneering work in several fields, but each had been founded (and was supported) to work only in its specialized field. Evangelicals were usually the major contributors and a majority of the members, but because of their single-function nature the associations did not represent the broader interests of evangelicals.

One early effort to offer an evangelical umbrella had limited success in the last half of the nineteenth century. Christian leaders from the United States and many other nations were invited to the organizational meeting of the Evangelical Alliance in London in 1846. It was to manifest Christian unity, sponsor a universal week of prayer, promote missions and revival, and assist churches under persecution. After the London meeting, the Americans sailed home eager to establish a branch in their country. But the timing was not right. Domestic politics preoccupied the nation. It was not until 1867, after the tragic and bloody war between North and South, that an American Alliance was constituted. Because there was little heart (or money) then for maintenance of anything not considered absolutely essential, the new evangelical body got off to a slow start.

The American Alliance lasted about forty years. One factor in its demise was the withdrawal of key leaders to participate in the newly formed Federal Council of Churches (FCC), which many evangelical leaders considered suspect if not actually heretical. Of particular concern to conservatives was an emphasis within the FCC on the "social gospel" as the mission of the church. Even though the Alliance had been given credit for raising the banner of Christian unity in modern times, the pull of the Federal Council with its claims to ecumenical leadership was stronger.

Despite dwindling American participation, British believers and colleagues mostly in their colonies kept the Alliance idea alive. The British unit took the ambitious name of the World's Evangelical Alliance.

Shock after shock in the early years of the twentieth century seemed to numb American Christians. Aside from some cooperative evangelistic campaigns and occasional ad hoc activities, little was accomplished toward large-scale evangelical cooperation. The battles with modernists were being fought in seminaries and denominations. World War I was a drain on Christian resources and compassion. Then there were the evolution debates, capped by the Scopes trial and its unflattering publicity for Bible believers. Wall Street's crash and the Depression took their toll, only to be followed by the rise of the Nazis in Europe and the prospect of another great war.

The New England Fellowship

One success story emerged in that troubled era. Surprisingly, it was in New England, a region sometimes written off as lost to the evangelical cause. J. Elwin Wright, a preacher's son of entrepreneurial bent, was the catalyst. His conference center at Rumney, New Hampshire, developed into a sort of New England evangelical headquarters. It brought into the area speakers of renown, and it sent out a variety of ministries into neighboring states (and beyond).

The first Rumney conference for pastors and other Christian workers brought together leaders from several denominations in 1929. Wright wrote afterwards that the August event in a big tent demonstrated that the pastors "could submerge their unessential differences and unite in perfect fellowship in a period of worship, spiritual inspiration, and prayer." Out of their fellowship and Wright's enthusiasm came the New England Fellowship (NEF). He described it as "a movement of great proportions and mighty possibilities." The movement, said the founder and first president, "is calling us to fellowship in Him regardless of our organic connections in spiritual work" and "to a spirit of humility and teachableness which will cause us to value all our brethren in Christ and to get their viewpoint without prejudice."

A ten-point doctrinal statement for NEF was approved. Its text was followed by this sentence: "These articles of faith are briefly summarized in the Apostles' Creed." In keeping with Wright's passion for emphasizing the things which unite instead of those which divide, it made no mention of the sacraments, mentioned the (invisible) church without saying what form the visible church should take, and affirmed the return of Christ without specifying any pattern for the last days. The officers endorsed the statement annually, and platform speakers at events were instructed to "offer nothing contrary to the spirit or letter" of it.

If the restatement of historic Christianity scared anyone away from participation, it wasn't recorded. To the contrary, the clear evangelical stand attracted supporters from within the region and without. A strong program was conducted through the depths of the Depression. The annual report for 1933, for example, reported an attendance of more than a thousand (from seventeen states) at three summer conferences, more than one hundred and fifty radio broadcasts on sixteen stations, twenty-one evangelistic campaigns or "extended Bible conferences" with ninety churches involved, 160 one-day campaigns or conferences with some eight hundred congregations cooperating, speakers at many other occasions, twenty thousand visits to distribute free literature, correspondence with "those needing spiritual advice and encouragement" and courses for daily vacation Bible school leaders and soul winners.

The Leadership of J. Elwin Wright

What happened officially under the NEF umbrella and what Wright the entrepreneur did personally was not always easy to distinguish. He was always on the move, full of ideas, and usually ahead of his time. The organization often didn't have the money to finance his projects, so he would put up the seed money himself. For many of the months that he was on the payroll as chief executive, he received only half salary or no salary at all. Income from real estate businesses in Florida and New Hampshire enabled him to live without the funds due him from the regional association.

Another of his commercial enterprises not officially related to NEF—but a part of his year-round ministry—was a bookstore in Orlando. He opened it in 1927 when Christian bookstores were few and far between. It helped set a pattern for an industry that would not develop rapidly across the nation until almost a half century later. However, his Florida success prompted him to open NEF bookstores at four locations across New England. One was at the busy Boston address: 5 Park Street (only a few steps from Park Street Church at "Brimstone Corner" and just up the street from Boston Common).

Before there was a national Youth For Christ (YFC) organization with Saturday night rallies in cities across the country, Wright had promoted ministry to young people. He started a regional program, named Youth for Christ, by the middle thirties. One of the guest speakers at the 1936 Rumney youth conference was a young pastor from Pittsburgh, Harold John Ockenga, later that year to become pastor at Park Street Church. Once a national YFC organization was launched, Wright attracted some of its leaders to New England. The Rumney 1948 program included the YFC evangelist, Billy Graham, whose name was not a household word until his 1949 Los Angeles crusade.

Day schools operated by evangelicals were also a rarity, especially in New England. That was all the more reason for Wright's initiatives. His chief assistant for many of his years with NEF was Elizabeth Evans, an education specialist. Together, they advised and encouraged groups of parents who wanted schools with a Christian basis for their children. When the first Boston area school borrowed to pay for its initial meeting place in 1946, two of the signatures on the loan were those of Wright (as a personal guarantor) and Miss Evans (as an officer of the school association).

Any list of Wright's interests would also include ministries of mercy—especially to neglected children. He ran an orphanage for First Fruit Harvesters Association, his father's ministry, and then pushed through the state legislature of New Hampshire a child welfare bill that was later considered a model in other states. In Florida, he organized missions to the children of migrant workers.

Cross Pollination

His reputation as a mover and shaker helped him bring to New England some of American's leading evangelicals. He put them on the Rumney summer conference programs, into missions conferences, on evangelistic circuits, and in big city rallies. Harry Rimmer came from California with his talks on science and faith. W. B. Riley, Minneapolis Baptist pastor and Northwestern Schools leader, preached at the first Rumney pastors' conference. Will Houghton came from Calvary Baptist Church of New York City in 1930, as did the Howard Taylors of China Inland Mission and Mrs. Charles Cowman, author of the devotional classic, *Streams in the Desert*. Radio pioneers Charles E. Fuller of "The Old Fashioned Revival Hour" and Walter Maier of "The Lutheran Hour" were booked for NEF events frequently. Missionaries from all over the world and from many sending societies were on Wright-arranged programs.

As his contacts increased, Wright's travels took him far beyond his Massachusetts and Florida bases. In 1937 he took the fellowship's Radio Ensemble (a musical group) on a twenty-nine state tour to the West Coast. On that trip he began to sense that

Christian leaders in other regions believed the nation should have something like the New England Fellowship. Hosts along the way encouraged him to explore the idea.

Pastors at the 1939 Rumney conference passed a resolution urging some kind of cooperative evangelical organization for the whole country. Similar resolutions were enacted the following two summers. There were also parallel movements. Ralph T. Davis, director of the Africa Inland Mission, wrote over the winter of 1940-41 to other mission leaders about the need for an organization to represent them before governments. He got favorable responses and his initiative was joined to Wright's. Wright organized another trip. . . .

2

A Committee Goes to Work

MANDATED BY HIS NEF BOARD and by the 1941 pastors' conference resolution to "take immediate steps" to "bring into existence a central and representative organization," Wright was off to Chicago. Will Houghton, then president of Moody Bible Institute, issued the invitations and convened a "round table discussion" on the proposition on October 27.

Wright was elected chairman quickly, and Ralph Davis, the Africa Inland Mission leader, was selected as secretary. Charles E. Fuller came, as did William Ward Ayer, another man who was making a name as a radio preacher from his pastorate at Calvary Baptist Church in New York. College presidents attending were V. Raymond Edman of Wheaton (Illinois) and Stephen W. Paine of Houghton (New York).

A Competing Option

While the idea for a national organization to represent evangelicals had been germinating for years and Wright and his NEF supporters had been talking about it actively for months, the meeting at Moody might have been easier to explain had it occurred six weeks earlier. That is because Carl McIntire formed his American Council of Christian Churches (ACCC) September 16. Initially, it was made up of two small denominations, but despite its size, it demanded attention because it came on the scene first. Wright had heard of McIntire's plan to organize and urged him to delay until after the October meeting in Chicago, but McIntire didn't wait. Nonetheless, he was still invited to the meeting at Moody, and he brought along two colleagues. But they took the occasion to invite the twelve or thirteen other men at the Chicago meeting to join *their* new council.

"Of the period spent by the brethren in session," say the minutes of the October 27-28 gathering, "about two-thirds of the time was devoted to counsel with the representatives of the above group." The American Council leaders explained that their organization would be comprised only of denominations which renounced all connection with the Federal

14

Council of Churches. During the long discussions, the group assembled by Houghton, Wright, and Davis determined that the main activity of the American Council would be opposing the Federal Council. While most of them had serious differences with the Federal Council, they believed any new association should have a more positive purpose than opposition to another group. There were other issues as well, including the fact that the ACCC was designed to encompass denominations only, leaving out the independent missions and other evangelical organizations in which most of them were involved. It would also close the door on individual believers and sympathetic congregations whose denominations did not join, for whatever reason. Wright was also concerned that McIntire's group might exclude Pentecostals.

Finally, the group decided that it would be "impossible for the rest of the brethren to unite" with the ACCC. The minutes record that McIntire and company then "felt there was nothing to be gained by their further presence" and left. They left, however, with an invitation from the initial planning group in Chicago to attend the organizational meeting which it planned for the following April in St. Louis.

Clarifying the Vision

The confrontation with the American Council organizers forced the other participants in the Chicago "round table" to the conviction "that God was leading them in a different direction," Miss Evans recalled.

15

In her book, *The Wright Vision,* she reported that they made a decision to invite to the St. Louis conference "leaders of Bible institutes, religious presses, and interdenominational organizations." While a general direction was now established, they were still open to "consider any suggestions," she noted.

Named to hear those ideas and to make concrete plans was a "temporary committee for united action among evangelicals." Its fourteen members, headed by Wright and Davis, included some others who were at the Chicago meeting and some who were not. Among the latter were pastor Harold Ockenga, Reformed Episcopal Bishop William Culbertson, Baptist editor John W. Bradbury, and missions leader Jacob Stam.

The first address for the temporary body was secretary Davis's Brooklyn address. There is a record of one "subcommittee" meeting there, with three members present. A half dozen other meetings, presumably with the full committee expected, were held in Manhattan (four of them at Calvary Baptist Church on West Fifty-seventh Street). Attendance ranged from five to nine.

Donald Grey Barnhouse, the Philadelphia Presbyterian pastor and radio expositor, was a guest at the first of the meetings November 10, 1941. His presence was another indication of Wright's openness and desire to include evangelicals in mainline churches as well as independents and those in conservative denominations. Barnhouse suggested a special effort to bring in Southern Baptists, Lutherans, and other Presbyterians, such as Clarence E. Macartney of Pittsburgh. The response to that suggestion was less than enthusiastic, the meeting's minutes said, and Barnhouse stayed only "a few moments."

The November meeting at Calvary Baptist was the last one before the nation was shaken by the December 7 attack on Pearl Harbor and carried into World War II. It could have been the last for the committee, but not with Wright at the helm. He was undeterred and considered the war another challenge and a new opportunity for ministry. Who, for instance, would furnish the chaplains for the military? A part of his effort would be to obtain commissions for evangelical ministers who wanted to serve in the military as chaplains.

A Public Invitation

Between meetings of the temporary committee, Wright worked hard at enlisting support for the cooperative idea and planning and publicizing the St. Louis organizational meetings. Over the winter of 1941-42 he toured the Midwest and the South. He conducted an extensive correspondence.

Soon he had 147 prominent leaders on the list of conveners of the April conference. The issuers of the public invitation were literally the "A to Z" of American evangelicalism. They were scattered all across the nation. They were laity and clergy. They represented a spectrum of denominational affiliations. Among the names on the alphabetical list were W. W. Ayer of Calvary Baptist, New York; L. Nelson Bell, Southern Presbyterian missionary home from China and the next year to become Billy Graham's father-in-law; Lewis Sperry Chafer of Dallas Seminary; Horace Dean of Philadelphia College of Bible; J. Roswell Flower, Assemblies of God executive; R. C. Grier, Associate Reformed Presbyterian leader; and Samuel Zwemer, revered apostle to the Muslim world.

Wright's reputation among evangelicals as a man who could get things done made it hard for anyone to turn down his requests for assistance. One of his claims to fame resulted from his association with broadcaster Charles E. Fuller. Wright and Fuller shared Vermont roots, but Fuller had never spoken in city-wide rallies east of Detroit, so Wright arranged meetings for him in Boston, New York, and Philadelphia. "The Old Fashioned Revival Hour" was broadcast live on 430 stations from those cities instead of from the usual origination point in Long Beach, California.

Wright Versus Little Caesar

But it was another kind of ability that Fuller sought when he called Wright one Monday morning from California. He asked the NEF president if he had noticed anything different about the music in that Sunday's broadcast of his program.

Elizabeth Evans, Wright's long-time assistant, recalled the conversation when Robert Shuster of the Billy Graham Center interviewed her in 1985 for the BGC archives: "Yes, I noticed there wasn't music," Wright had said. "What happened?"

Fuller replied that his musicians and the network were the target of a union organizing effort by the American Federation of Musicians and its colorful president, James Caesar Petrillo. The labor leader told the coast-to-coast preacher that all of his singers and instrumentalists would have to join the union. If not, he promised, the program would be put off the air.

"I can not do it," Fuller declared. "Conscientiously, I can not do it. These are all volunteers. Nobody is paid any salary, and they don't believe in the union, and they can't afford to join the union [and pay dues] just to sing in my choir on Sunday evening."

The labor boss was just as adamant. He promised the preacher, "All right, you won't have any music on Sunday night."

When the nation's favorite evangelistic broadcaster reached Wright Monday morning, he asked the New England "doer" to "please look after it."

Wright took off for Washington immediately. Among his stops was one at the office of a senior senator, who heard the story with interest.

"He's gotten too big, and we've just been waiting for a good chance to put him down in his place," the senator said. He told Wright that Petrillo had even blocked a scheduled Marine Band performance at a special benefit, and that the president had backed down lest he run afoul of organized labor.

"We will get right at it in the Senate," the powerful legislator promised. "You tell him that if he doesn't do differently, why we'll have a Senate investigation."

There was no government action. It was not necessary. Petrillo backed off when Wright got word to him that he was in danger of being quizzed under oath, with the attendant publicity.

The next Sunday the "Old Fashioned Revival Hour" choir was again singing "Heavenly Sunshine" on America's airwaves.

Evangelicals had no official representation in Washington then, but with this case, Wright highlighted the need and demonstrated how something *could* be done. Not only was the famed "Little Caesar" of the musicians' union going after gospel broadcasters, but they also felt pressure from the networks, the Federal Council of Churches, and the Federal Communications Commission. The NEF president thought there were at least eight million evangelicals unrepresented in the corridors of power and that Washington should hear their voice.

"It was a strong point in favor of starting a National Association of Evangelicals," Miss Evans remembered.

3

The Spirit of St. Louis

WERE THERE REALLY TWENTY MILLION evangelicals in America at the beginning of World War II? Unorganized—or disorganized—as they were, no one really knew.

Elizabeth Evans recalled, however, that "Charles Fuller fully realized . . . that there were about eight million people listening to Charles Fuller." The growing Southern Baptist constituency probably overlapped somewhat that of "The Old Fashioned Revival Hour," but it might have added others as well. Then there were "The Lutheran Hour" loyalists and other ethnically-based communities such as the Dutch Reformed. Black believers were also numerous, especially in Baptist and Pentecostal groups.

Not everyone was convinced. One of those who received special attention from Wright was Harold John Ockenga, then of Park Street Church, Boston.

"He was fairly new in New England," Miss Evans recalled in her interview for the archives. "I think he did not fully sense the disagreements, or the lack of unity, the lack of working together, or perhaps the need for it. He might not realize the value of speaking for eight million people."

But he became convinced. He was put on the program of the St. Louis conference as the keynoter. His topic: "The Unvoiced Multitudes." Ockenga pulled out all the stops. The master orator left no question that he favored a new organization to lift the evangelical banner in the United States.

First, though, he paid high tribute to Wright. He acknowledged Wright's influence on his thinking and that of many others. "I have long since come to learn that whenever Mr. Wright believes that a movement will be a success, it will be a success," Ockenga explained. "I wish to pay tribute also to the manner in which he has steered this spontaneous movement between the rocks of middle-of-the-roadism and fanaticism. Mr. Wright has demonstrated true statesmanship, and I think we will do well to follow his leadership."

The Spirit's Leading

The prominent Boston pastor's address was not the first item on the conference program. The night before (April 6), about forty early registrants set the tone for the meeting. They gathered for a preliminary prayer time, in which, according to the official record, "The spirit of the Lord was very graciously present, and the fellowship in prayer was inspiring."

Private recollections reinforced that assessment. William R. Nicholl, pastor of the First United Presbyterian Church, Quincy, Massachusetts, wrote, "While attending the conference I was impressed with the fact that the movement was the direct leading of the Holy Spirit. This was especially manifested by the prayerful and thoughtful attitude of all the delegates, who had no special interests of their own as they sought to know the mind of Christ."

Returning from St. Louis to his duties as president of Gordon College, Nathan R. Wood wrote, "There was an atmosphere of prayer without ceasing." There was very evident on the part of all the forces which were shaping the movement a humility and a waiting upon God which deeply impressed many of us. It was not our modern western world in its usual mode of organization. Rather, it reminded us of the New Testament councils where there was one Leader."

The next morning, with about 150 present, the meeting was called to order officially by Elwin Wright at 9:30 a.m., Tuesday, April 7, 1942. It was the week after Easter and only four months after the Japanese attack at Pearl Harbor. The meeting was in the Hotel Coronado, not far from Union Station, the railway crossroads of the United States. The trains were packed with passengers whose lives were being abruptly changed by the war. Delegates to the evangelical conference sensed they were at an important crossroads.

After opening devotions, led by Herbert E. Kann, a minister from Buffalo, New York, Wright sketched the background of the movement, read the call to the meeting, and expressed his hopes for it. He emphasized the seriousness of the moment and the need for prayerful consideration: "We do urge the need of much prayer and careful study at every stage of the proceedings, for upon the decisions made here may rest the course of evangelical effort in this country for many years to come."

The temporary committee, Wright reported, had been "bound together in a delightful and harmonious fellowship," with all of its decisions made unanimously. He said he and the other members considered that their work was completed and that the assembled delegates had a clean slate before them: "Without exception, the members of the committee have served without desiring to be considered for any place of prominence in whatever organization may eventually result from your deliberations. Each of us is fully occupied in his own field of labor to which the Lord has called him and would not wish to accept any office in connection with such an organization. Therefore, this conference is in a position to decide upon its procedure and leadership without the embarrassment of any cut-and-dried plan regarding the form of organization or the personnel of its officers, staff and committees."

Handicapped by the lack of any inclusive national listing of evangelical organizations, the temporary committee's chairman explained, his office sent invitations to all the groups known to him. It was the intention of the planners, according to Wright, to provide all interested bodies "a fair opportunity to start together from the very foundation to build the sort of organization which, in their united judgment, under the guidance of the Holy Spirit, would answer the need."

A Cross Section of Evangelicals

With Wright's gifts for promotion and publicity, it's likely that few significant evangelical groups were unaware of the open invitation. If any interested people were not at the St. Louis meeting, it was probably because of wartime travel restrictions or something other than lack of information. Those who attended came from all over the map—ecclesiastically as well as geographically. They represented a cross section of the "unvoiced multitudes" who thought evangelicals had something to say to the nation.

From Granite City, Illinois, came a young Assemblies of God pastor named Thomas Zimmerman— later to be the top executive of his denomination and NAE's longest-serving leader. Industrialist H. J. Taylor came from Chicago. J. O. Buswell, then president of the National Bible Institute of New York, registered. Another venerable leader of conservative forces on the roster was David Otis Fuller, the Grand Rapids, Michigan, Baptist preacher. Cornelius Van Til, the philosopher-apologete, came from Westminster Seminary in Philadelphia.

Among the handful traveling from the West were: Harry B. Ansted, Free Methodist official in Seattle; G. B. Huebert of Reedley, California, general conference moderator of the Mennonite Brethren Church; and R. L. Decker, Baptist pastor in Fort Collins, Colorado.

There were delegates from Cleveland, Ohio, and Cleveland, Tennessee. Others registered from Fort Wayne, Indiana, and Fort Worth, Texas. They came from East St. Louis, Illinois, and Due West, South Carolina, as well as Minneapolis and Miami. Leaders from the Christian and Missionary Alliance, the Salvation Army, the Church of God (Cleveland), the Pilgrim Holiness Church, the Wesleyan Methodist Church, and several other denominations were on hand. Other individuals attended without any of the officials from their denominations. A variety of independent ministries was represented.

No one participated as an official representative of his or her organization, however. The temporary committee had decided that waiting on all possible interested bodies to elect *formally* their representatives would delay progress. Instead, the panel decided on the April 1942 conference to launch the association and a 1943 constitutional convention which would, in effect, confirm the initial decisions and receive the reports from denominations and other organizations which wanted to join on the basis of those initial decisions.

A Keynote that Was in Tune

Whether those attending the St. Louis meeting were high officials in their organizations or lonely pastors, Ockenga established rapport with them quickly in his keynote address.

"I, myself, am one of the unvoiced multitude," he said as he began. "I represent Mr. John Q. [Public] of the clergy, or, if you please, one of the unrepresented preachers in the concerted movements of our day. You may be sure that I keenly feel this position of a lone wolf, as I have sometimes been called, but I recognize that there are many lone wolves in the ministry today who in a measure have been greatly blessed by God in their own particular fields of endeavor. Yet I see on the horizon ominous clouds of battle which spell annihilation unless we are willing to run in a pack."

Ockenga suggested that evangelical loneliness was no new phenomenon: "Evangelical Christianity has suffered nothing but a series of defeats for decades. The programs of few major denominations today are controlled by evangelicals. Evangelical testimony has sometimes been reduced to the witness of individual churches. New England is an example of this sad situation. Evangelicals, one after another, have been so frozen out that the territory is almost a mission field . . . evangelically an arid waste."

The keynoter warned his war-conscious audience that fellow believers were in a position similar to that of small nations in the path of the rampaging German and Japanese military machines.

"One by one," the Boston pastor declared, "various forces have discredited or attacked them, or even forced them out of positions of leadership, until today many of them are on the defensive or even the decline. The hour calls for united front for evangelical action."

The Folly of Disunity

He cited his own experience checking out the radio situation. Ockenga reported that after corresponding with some of the top gospel broadcasters, he got in touch with executives of the National Broadcasting Company (the NBC network). Finally, there was a six hour Boston meeting with a network executive and the manager of its affiliate in the city, WBZ. He learned there, the pastor said, "we shall have absolutely no opportunity of sharing equally in the broadcasting facilities of that great company" unless evangelicals organize nationally.

"We are a very large minority, perhaps a majority, in America, which is discriminated against because of the folly of our divided condition," Ockenga asserted.

NBC's policy was to recognize three faith groups: Catholic, Protestant, and Jewish, and to divide its sustaining (free) time religious programs between them. The trouble with that, from the evangelical point of view, was that NBC considered the Federal Council of Churches as the sole representative of Protestantism. The network refused to sell time to religious broadcasters, so those not picked by the Federal Council had no access to NBC. The Columbia Broadcasting System (CBS) had a similar policy. The third major radio network of that day, Mutual, sold some time (to Charles E. Fuller, among others), but it was sending signals that it might stop that practice.

Not only were evangelicals losing out in radio, but Ockenga pointed to education and other areas where leadership was in other hands.

"Look about you at individuals in our churches," the keynoter urged. "They are defeated, reticent, retiring and seemingly in despair. . . . This sense of isolation and impotency on the part of individuals has driven them into corporate organizations with a strong central governing power."

Standing Together

Ockenga suggested that the dispirited believers could find hope and power for their cause in spiritual unity.

"This means," he cautioned, "that this millstone of rugged independency which has held back innumerable movements before, in which individual leaders must be the whole hog or none, must be utterly repudiated by every one of us." Along with that unity, Ockenga urged purity and love—"consecrated love" of the brethren.

He did not coin the term, "silent majority," which was to become important in American politics decades later, but his speaking for what he considered to be a majority struck a chord with evangelicals. The Boston pastor was followed to the lectern by William Ward Ayer, the New York preacher whose offices at Calvary Baptist Church had been the scene of most of the planning committee's meetings. In his speech, Ayer reiterated Ockenga's warnings that fragmentation was a hazard to virile evangelicalism.

"Millions of evangelical Christians," Ayer suggested, "if they had a common voice and a common meeting place, would exercise under God an influence that would save American democracy."

Next at the lectern was the scholarly Stephen W. Paine, president of Houghton College. He picked up on the theme of united action but warned against uniting only to oppose other forces. "Negative motives for united action contain within themselves the very seeds of disintegration," Paine warned. "They are centrifugal, and as soon as the immediate pressure is lessened, the supposed unity of action flies to the four points of the compass."

30

4

A Fundamental Discussion

THOSE SOBERING MESSAGES on the first morning of the St. Louis conference set the stage for actions that followed. Just before Paine spoke, a motion was approved authorizing Wright to name three members to a committee that would propose larger committees on agenda and nominations. They returned at the end of the Paine address and suggested seven members for each of the panels, and they were elected.

The nominating committee got to work immediately and came into the plenary after the lunch break with its choices for temporary officers. R. G. Lee, the Southern Baptist pulpiteer from Memphis, was recommended for chairman and elected. The conference accepted the recommendation that its keynoter, Harold Ockenga, be vice-chairman.

Lee took the gavel, and the conference began its first consideration of business.

But now what?

Delegates had no dockets, and Wright had insisted that no "cut-and-dried plan" of work had been decided by the organizers. He was called to the platform for suggestions. He repeated his statement that his temporary committee had finished its job when the conference elected its own officers. Now, he said, he and his colleagues would prefer to stay in the background and allow the delegates to chart their own course. There were, he suggested, the general areas of missions, radio, and other matters of interest.

McIntire's Second Pitch

Apparently of more immediate interest was Carl McIntire and his American Council of Christian Churches. He had indeed accepted the invitation of the temporary committee to attend, and he was present with a group of his supporters—several from the St. Louis area. And he was ready to speak. He did. He wanted these evangelicals in the ACCC and said so plainly. He saw no reason for two national organizations. The founding principles of his council were not negotiable, however. Nearly a half century later he told an interviewer that he did leave open the possibility of another name if the group represented in St. Louis did not like ACCC.

Some in the audience did not know McIntire. Others knew him very well. He and Ockenga had been classmates, and he had been in Ockenga's wedding. Ockenga, who had kept up with his activities over the years, only that morning had clearly called for another organization—not for affiliation with his old friend's council.

The official record of the first business session reported the decision diplomatically but succinctly: "After listening to Mr. McIntire's statement, the conference voted to proceed to the consideration of such an organization as would be in keeping with the purposes and policies embodied in the call sent out by the temporary committee."

In making that decision, the delegates followed the lead of the temporary committee at its initial meeting at Moody Bible Institute the previous October. That first planning group had, in effect, told McIntire that it was interested in more than an instrument for protesting the Federal Council.

While the American Council leaders were unknown to some of the delegates, the issue of joining forces with them was not. No one was surprised when McIntire showed up at the Hotel Coronado. He was expected to push his cause forcefully. Since the meeting was open to anyone who wanted to register, the makeup of the assembly was uncertain. In addition to members of his own denomination who accompanied him, McIntire had other supporters among the participants. The issue was his doctrine of separation, and some of them promoted its acceptance by the new organization just as vigorously as he did. The ACCC leader at that point would not consider fellowship with any person, congregation, or conference of churches maintaining a connection with a denomination in the Federal Council. He called for the faithful to break away from those denominations.

Seeking a Positive Identity

In contrast, the group meeting in St. Louis decided to receive as members congregations, conferences, and other organizations that would accept the statement of faith. (Later, individual nonvoting memberships would also be offered.)

"We should be able to at least shake hands over the tops of the fences," Wright often said of fellow believers, according to Miss Evans. His New England Fellowship, which had impressed so many, emphasized building unity among Christians. His organization had made a point of not encouraging lonely evangelicals to leave their churches. Instead, it brought them together with others of like mind for inspiration and fellowship. In NEF they also found outreach programs they could support.

During the St. Louis debate, David Otis Fuller, the prominent Baptist preacher from Grand Rapids, proposed that the new organization be limited to groups which, if connected to the Federal Council, had gone on record repudiating that body. The majority voted against that concept.

"It should be pointed out that there was no assurance that if Dr. Fuller's proposal at St. Louis had been adopted, the men of the ACCC would have been satisfied with such a repudiation in the place of full and complete 'separation,'" Stephen Paine wrote later. In his 1951 booklet, *"Separation"—Is Separating Evangelicals,* Paine took McIntire to task for inconsistencies in his own application of the separation doctrine. At the same time, he emphasized that NAE consistently stood for orthodox belief and against apostasy.

"The feeling of the NAE men has been that our organization was not founded to fight anybody, and as far as the Federal Council is concerned," declared Paine, "the very fact of our establishing this new organization in our constitution 'against the apostasy of groups claiming to represent Protestant Christianity without such loyalty to the historic gospel of the Lord Jesus Christ (Article IIa)' should make our position clear to anyone who was sincerely wondering where we stood."

Repudiation or denunciation, he concluded, was not the issue. It was absolute separation and joining McIntire's council.

That was not an attractive option for most of the participants in the conference. Perhaps to prove the point, the people they elected to govern the association until the 1943 constitutional convention represented a broad denominational spectrum. Heading the list as the first president was Ockenga, a Presbyterian then technically on loan to a Congregational church.

In a testimony published shortly after the conference, Howard W. Ferrin, president of the Providence (Rhode Island) Bible Institute, summed up the St. Louis accomplishments: "Here is no movement which will be too limited in its fellowship to be effective, or too broad in its doctrinal position to be ineffective."

Another educational institution's president with unquestioned credentials as a theological conservative, Lewis Sperry Chafer of Dallas Seminary, also praised the decision. He wrote shortly after participating in the conference that it was "in itself a genuine achievement and all conservative Christians may take heart in the fact that so much was accomplished in the direction of a permanent organization of evangelicals."

Chafer's endorsement was straight to the point on the course chosen at St. Louis: "Some of us feel deeply the need of fellowship and the zest of partnership in prosecuting a constructive testimony for Christ. I believe our first obligation is in the line of positive proclamation of God's truth rather than a negative objection against some specific enemy." Then, remarkably, he invoked the name of his mentor: "Dr. C. I. Scofield's counsel, given to me on his deathbed, has molded my own life and is to the point here, namely: 'Never descend to mere controversy. You have no time or strength for that. Give out the positive Word. Nothing can stand before it.'"

Without naming McIntire, the Dallas Seminary chief took verbal aim: "There are types of minds, however sincere, that seem to believe Christian service consists in attacking some entrenched foe, and if that effort does not occupy all their time they must attack other Christians who are led to work in a more constructive way. These are sometimes held up to scorn. There is need of an organization which is formed to declare God's truth to a lost world rather than to attack other lines of Christian work. In due time steps may need to be taken in the direction of exposing that which is false. A man and a woman may be united in marriage for mutual benefit. However, it would be unworthy for either one to enter that union merely to prosecute a conflict with a mother-in-law."

Wright Recruited

While they no doubt appreciated Chafer's view as well as his illustration, the cautious organizers of the conference were not prepared to pronounce consummation of a union. They had stressed all along that any results of the St. Louis meeting would be submitted to interested churches, who would in turn decide the next year to make it official if that is what they wanted. A constitutional convention was called for the next spring in Chicago.

And Wright, who had said he did not want a job other than the one he had with the New England Fellowship, was persuaded to be the first executive, initially with the title of promotional secretary. He set up shop in an office in Park Street Church, and his promotional literature bore the address of Zero Park Street, Boston, Massachusetts. It was considered a half-time job, and he continued as NEF's president. The regional organization continued to flourish, so its board hired a minister to assist Wright, giving him the title of executive secretary. The minister didn't join the NEF staff officially until April 1943, however, so Wright ran the day-to-day operations of both groups for a full year.

5

The Galvanizing Issue

NEVER ONE TO LET THE GRASS GROW where he stood, Wright began his NAE assignment immediately. He planned a series of regional conferences to take the St. Louis message closer to the grass roots. The first was in New York June 8. He started making arrangements for the 1943 constitutional convention. He put together a book, *Evangelical Action*, about the organizing conference.

Before the new National Association of Evangelicals for United Action (the name adopted in St. Louis) was a month old, Wright was in action on a national platform in its behalf. The issue which helped galvanize and unite evangelicals across the country was access to the air waves. Wright and a couple of representatives of the Moody Bible Institute's radio ministry attended an annual event (May 3–6, 1942) at Ohio State University (Columbus) called the Institute for Education by Radio. Wright was given the opportunity to speak at the section on religious radio.

Since the meeting in St. Louis, he told the delegates, there was a new boy on the block.

"We favor a fair division of time between representatives of the principal faiths for sustaining broadcasts," he explained, "but we believe there should be four rather than three faiths taken into consideration. Besides the Catholics and Jews, we have two great divisions of the church, probably of approximately equal numerical strength. The first is represented by the Federal Council of the Churches of Christ in America. This includes the so-called liberal or modernist groups. The second is the evangelical or conservative group, which, up to the present time, has been without cohesion and consequently without representation. The National Association of Evangelicals for United Action seems likely to become the representative of this group of between fifteen and twenty million church members, including practically all Protestant groups not in the membership of the Federal Council, also a large number of individual churches within denominations which are members of the Federal Council, but not sympathetic to its program."

His estimates might have been high, but the first NAE executive was careful to note that the organization was still in formation. The newly-born association "will remain in a somewhat fluid state" until formally constituted in 1943, he suggested to the radio specialists at Columbus.

Freedom to Preach with Conviction

Meanwhile, Wright told his audience, "I will endeavor to present what I believe to be the consensus of opinion of leading evangelicals" (on the topics before the institute). Five formal recommendations were under consideration, and Wright took issue with four of them.

He said the people he represented could "heartily agree" with the proposal that "religious programs should not attack the beliefs of members of other faiths." To use the electronic media otherwise, he declared, would be in "exceedingly bad taste."

But the NAE executive secretary (as he was being called increasingly) attacked the first of the recommendations as an unnecessary dilution of sincere convictions. It called for all programs to be addressed to "a cross section of the public" and "not to members of any one faith." Wright said that if the intent was to so water down content that broadcasts "will cease to have the power to bring conviction of spiritual need," then evangelicals would be opposed. He explained, "We believe that this is a matter of eternal life or death whether men accept Jesus Christ as

41

Deity and the only Saviour of mankind. Believing this we would be lacking in sincerity, as you can understand, I am sure, if we failed to do all in our power to win men to faith in Christ by the preaching of His Gospel." Wright added that evangelicals were prepared to defend the rights of Catholics and Jews to use their broadcasts "to be just as positive in their programs as we wish to be in ours."

Free Time vs. Paid Time

The other recommendations on religious programs facing the radio "clearing house" at Columbus were all related to the big question of free time versus paid time and the allocation of those hours.

"We entirely disagree," Wright insisted, with the elimination of paid religious broadcasting. NBC and CBS had "almost entirely excluded" from their network programs "doctrinally conservative groups," he pointed out. He suggested that if the rest of the industry (individual stations as well as the other network, Mutual) were allowed to follow their example the result would be a virtual absence of evangelical voices on the air.

NAE's first staff member pressed his point: "The broadcasting companies are not likely to be willing to contribute the amount of time which the presentation of religion deserves and requires. We believe that groups financially able to carry a broadcast should be permitted to buy time. There are many organizations which can and will pay for time if given a reasonable opportunity for the recovery of the cost."

On the matter of sustaining time, Wright acknowledged that "the broadcast companies cannot be expected to deal with two hundred or more separate organizations" in allotting the free hours. Removing that obstacle was one of the main reasons for formation of NAE, he noted: "In order to secure recognition, we have organized that we may have a voice in radio and in other matters of common interest and concern."

Offering the industry a "fourth force" with which to deal did not solve all the problems, however. Wright made clear that even if evangelicals were treated fairly in the distribution of sustaining time programs they also wanted a fair shake at buying time. One of the recommendations before the Columbus conference was worded to say that religious programs, "like educational broadcasts," should be aired on a sustaining basis. The feisty New Englander shot that down quickly by pointing out that time was purchased for many "educational" shows.

The infant association's spokesman then confronted the fairness of the proposed ban on the solicitation of contributions.

Freedom to Solicit Contributions

"If a broadcaster is paying for time," he reasoned, "it is only reasonable that opportunity be given to the listeners to share in the expense. One might as reasonably say to a commercial broadcaster, 'You may not directly or indirectly offer your product for sale.' Or to the American Red Cross, 'You may tell about the work of the Red Cross but no mention must be made of paying one dollar for an annual membership.'"

Wright pointed out that listeners to evangelical programs tune in because they expect to derive benefit. In the same way that people attending church services are invited to help defray the costs, radio listeners may be asked to share in the expenses of the program, he said. The NAE representative, in the best American tradition, stressed that both tuning in and making contributions were voluntary: "There is certainly no compulsion about it."

One reason given for the proposed prohibition of on-air solicitation was the existence of some unscrupulous profiteers. Wright hit that issue head-on and made clear where responsible Christians stood.

He declared: "There is undoubtedly a good deal of racketeering going on in connection with religious broadcasts and that racketeering is almost wholly confined to a certain type of program which is undesirable from every standpoint. We are desirous of giving full cooperation in curbing such programs without injury to legitimate broadcasts. As a means of attaining that end, we suggest that broadcasts for which payment is made be confined to established churches or incorporated organizations approved by one of the groups previously mentioned [NAE or one

of the other three major faiths]. This would eliminate practically all broadcasts conducted for personal profit."

After admitting knowledge of some unethical operators in the field and indicating a willingness to
help clean them out, the NAE staffer frankly indicated that he was suspicious that the proposed solicitation ban was directed "not only against racketeering broadcasters but [also against] others which provide no reasonable grounds for complaint." He continued, "If there is insistence that the broadcasting
of religious programs for which payment is made be
discontinued, or that restrictions be imposed which
will prevent a dignified financial appeal, I am here
to warn you that there will be a protest on the part of
millions of listeners in every section of the country
such as has not been heard since broadcasting was
inaugurated."

Lest they focus all their attention on the shady
characters in religious radio, Wright called attention
to the record of his friend, Charles E. Fuller of the
"Old Fashioned Revival Hour." The NAE spokesman
asserted, "I happen to know, for instance, that 94.5
percent of all offerings received by the 'Old Fashioned Revival Hour' go directly for payment of station time and only 5.5 percent for office overhead,
salaries and other incidental expenses—a remarkable record."

Wright could give those specific figures without
fear of contradiction because of his New England

reputation for pinching pennies and for accounting to his constituency for his stewardship. Long before many other religious organizations did so, his New England Fellowship had a board audit committee that reviewed the financial records annually. His own relationship to Fuller was such that it would not be considered unusual for him to walk into the Fuller organization's office and ask to see the books. He and the leading evangelical broadcaster of that day knew they were in a spiritual battle, and the last thing they needed was a scandal within the camp about mishandling of money.

Win Some, Lose Some

As hard as it tried, the NAE delegation at the 1942 session of the Institute for Education by Radio did not win all the points it attempted to make. It won some and lost some. The main loss was on the recommendation to ban on-air solicitation. Here is how that was explained in the executive committee's published report: "In view of the fact that the recommendations are not necessarily binding upon the stations, it is felt that there may be a later chance to review this recommendation."

The stations across the nation were, in fact, not bound, and many continued to offer a place on their schedules to preachers who asked for financial support.

Even though the Columbus "clearing house" did not agree with NAE on the solicitation issue, a couple of the other recommendations that Wright opposed were voted down.

"The greatest gain" at the Ohio State meeting, the association's report stated, "was the unanimous agreement on the part of the various representatives of religious faiths and of the broadcasting companies that evangelicals should have a fair allotment of time on sustaining programs over the networks, now that they are in a position to speak through a central organization."

Participants in the institute also agreed that some time should be available for purchase and that evangelicals had a right to voice their convictions on the air "without dilution."

Why did Wright devote so much time and energy so early in NAE's life to the radio question? It was, first of all, the point at which Bible-believing Christians throughout the country thought their freedom was most at risk. Moreover, in the words of the official report on the NAE delegation's work in Columbus, "it is illustrative of the vast amount of constructive work which may be accomplished" by the fledgling association.

6

The Constitutional Convention

AS SPRING TURNED TO SUMMER in 1942, American
involvement in the war touched nearly every
family. Military volunteers, as well as the draftees,
left home for training—and battle. Children helped
collect scrap metal to aid the war effort. People
learned to live on the limited quantities of rationed
commodities. Educations were interrupted. Gold
stars began to appear on little flags in living room
windows, indicating that a son died in his country's
defense.

Pastors were busy. The nation, just emerging
from the Depression, faced a new emergency. Congregations turned to prayer.

Everyone was preoccupied with war news, but the leaders of the new NAE believed they should continue the work they were instructed to do by the St. Louis conference. Military enlistees signed up "for the duration," but nobody knew then how long the war would last. Postponing the formal organization of the new association was not an appealing idea. The idea of doing so smacked of putting it off indefinitely. These men were committed to each other and to meeting a need, so they pressed ahead.

Wright's fabled ability to build something of value from minimal materials was tested severely. He was trying to set up a new national organization of civilians at a time when top priority went to the military. Even train tickets sometimes required special permission. To get speakers to meetings or bring his planning committee together, Wright had to fill out detailed forms or at times meet with government bureaucrats just to arrange transportation.

NAE officers and their sole staffer worked through the summer and fall of 1942, leading regional meetings, accepting other opportunities to speak about NAE, and meeting denominational leaders. They wrote articles, and they corresponded with the potential supporters they were unable to meet face-to-face.

Bathed in Prayer

Prayer was emphasized during this preparatory period. Prayer got top billing in the call to the constitutional convention. NAE's temporary leaders requested "earnest intercessory prayer for a new infilling of the Spirit upon every delegate." They also asked sympathetic churches to make May 2 a special day of prayer and to ask their members to pray daily during the convention, starting May 3, 1943.

The prayers were answered. Attendance zoomed from the previous year's 150 to about a thousand at the Chicago convention. The registrants came from a wider denominational spectrum than the previous year. In a 1956 history, James DeForest Murch reckoned that "in one way or another" they represented fifty denominations "with a potential constituency of fifteen million."

Not only were the numbers heartening to the leaders who had worked and prayed for a year, but so was the atmosphere. Some two-hundred early arrivals gathered for a preliminary prayer meeting. Murch reported later that "the presence of God was evident to every heart" and that the time was "akin to Pentecost."

Robert C. McQuilkin, the first president of Columbia (South Carolina) Bible College and no Pentecostal, explained: "Probably no convention in many years of church history gave such a demonstration of the unity of the Spirit in great fundamentals of the faith along with many varieties of Christian experience and Bible interpretation. . . ."

Dale Cryderman, a youth worker for the Free Methodist Church, had this impression: "As one of the younger delegates present, it was a definite blessing to observe the spirit of humility and Christian love as evidenced in the lives of those taking part in the Chicago convention. Two events stand out in my mind and will not soon be erased. They are the opening prayer service held the first evening and the closing hour of the convention with the entire body kneeling in a spirit of prayer, melted by the influence of God into one unit for His cause."

Cryderman's impression lasted, as did his interest in NAE. He worked in the organization throughout his ministerial career of more than forty years. As a former newspaper photographer, Cryderman initially helped with news room operation at the association's conventions.

Leading the news room work at the Chicago convention was a young former reporter named Carl F. H. Henry who was in his first year as a fulltime professor at Northern Baptist Seminary. It was also in 1943 that Zondervan published the first of his many books, a church publicity handbook. Theologian Henry, who was to become one of the evangelical world's giants over the following decades, was particularly well suited for the job of reporting the Chicago deliberations because a key decision was theological.

Seven Essential Points

The prototype New England Fellowship had a ten-point doctrinal statement, and Elwin Wright emphasized in his introductory remarks at the 1942 conference in St. Louis that the new association should make a strong declaration of faith. A compact version of the NEF document was adopted in 1942, but that was one of the decisions that many delegates wanted to consider more thoroughly before the constitution was adopted in 1943. Did the St. Louis statement not say enough? Or did it say more than the full convention could accept?

"Some pessimists declared that the convention would never be able to agree unitedly to any statement that might be devised," Murch recalled more than a decade after NAE's formation. "But there was a strange moving of the Spirit of God which brought agreement with a minimum of discussion."

Adopted—without dissent—was a seven-point doctrinal affirmation that would not only be NAE's standard, but it also became the official statement of faith for many independent, interdenominational evangelical organizations in the years which followed.

While the finally-approved seven points were very similar to those adopted the year before, there were differences. The 1942 drafters began each article with the word "that," and it was dropped in the 1943 version. Instead, each one started simply, "We believe . . ."

With the exception of the deletion of that single word, the first article remained exactly as before, affirming the bedrock belief in the Bible. It says:

I. We believe the Bible to be the inspired, the only infallible, authoritative Word of God.

With that foundation established, the statement then goes on to assert other cardinal points of historic Christianity. Second, and with no substantive difference, was the article on the Trinity:

II. We believe that there is one God, eternally existent in three persons: Father, Son and Holy Spirit.

Amendments were made on the third article, on Christ. It was expanded from the 1942 effort by explicit reference to the Lord's shed blood and by use of the fuller term "our Lord Jesus Christ," instead of simply "Christ." As adopted, it reads:

III. We believe in the deity of our Lord Jesus Christ, in His virgin birth, in His sinless life, in His miracles, in His vicarious and atoning death through His shed blood, in His bodily resurrection, in His ascension to the right hand of the Father, and in His personal return in power and glory.

The fourth point, somewhat reduced from the 1942 draft, which had been prefaced with a reference to "the exceeding sinfulness of human nature," says:

IV. We believe that for the salvation of lost and sinful man, regeneration by the Holy Spirit is absolutely essential.

A new article was added by the constitutional convention to emphasize the ministry of the Holy Spirit beyond regeneration. Point five reads:

V. We believe in the present ministry of the Holy Spirit by whose indwelling the Christian is enabled to live a godly life.

No substantive changes were made in the final two articles approved in 1942.

VI. We believe in the resurrection of both the saved and the lost; that they are saved unto the resurrection of life and they that are lost unto the resurrection of damnation.

VII. We believe in the spiritual unity of believers in our Lord Jesus Christ.

Officers and Board Members

Besides settling the theological basis, the convention approved other constitutional provisions. Succeeding conventions were authorized to elect a panel of five officers plus a board of administration of twenty to forty members. That board would meet twice a year. It would elect six members to serve with the officers as an executive committee, with that body being given broad powers to supervise the work of the association and to act between conventions and meetings of the board.

Under the new constitution, the first president was Harold Ockenga. Having served a year under the provisional rules and then a year under the new document, his total term at the NAE helm was two years. That precedent has been followed ever since, and all the presidents have served two years.

At St. Louis, a Southern Baptist minister from Memphis, R. J. Bateman, was elected first vice-president. At the 1943 Chicago convention he was replaced by Free Methodist Bishop Leslie R. Marston, who moved up from second vice-president. Thus, the association put Marston in line to succeed Ockenga the next year. That began a tradition of alternating the top office between members of different doctrinal families, with Ockenga representing the Reformed perspective and Marston the Wesleyan.

A layman who was chairman of Bateman's First Baptist board of deacons, Judge John W. McCall, was elected second vice-president. A prominent Philadelphia lawyer, J. Willison Smith, Jr., was elected secretary, and Chicago industrialist H. J. Taylor accepted another term as treasurer.

Elwin Wright, ready again to return to his New England Fellowship duties, was asked to stay another year as the NAE executive. He accepted the call, this time with the official title of field secretary.

Men elected to the executive committee and board of administration came from all parts of the country (and one from Canada) and from a cross section of denominational life. Most were ministers. Among the few laymen on the executive committee was Kenneth S. Keyes. This Miami real estate tycoon went to the Chicago convention at the invitation of his Presbyterian pastor, Daniel Iverson, who had been an early advocate of the new body. Iverson served on the Committee of Twenty-five (precursor of the board of administration) in the year following the St. Louis conference, but like Bateman, the Memphis Baptist, he apparently stepped aside to push one of his laymen into a position of leadership.

The laity were better represented on the National Advisory Committee of Twenty-three. Among them were Chattanooga educator J. P. McCallie and Northwest timber baron C. Davis Weyerhauser. One woman, Mrs. Phillip Armour III, was elected to the advisory group.

"An impressive feature of the convention," Murch reported, "was the spirit of fairness shown in the wording of the constitution, in the debates, and in the consideration given the smaller denominations in the selection of association leadership."

Commissioned for Action

Also impressive was a proposed program of "united evangelical action" recommended by the convention's committee on policy and fields of endeavor. The panel was not timid about taking on the world in its list, but Murch noted that members "appreciated the fact that their proposals to the Chicago convention were largely tentative and would be modified or enlarged as time and experience and the leadership of the Spirit would determine."

Missions, evangelism, radio, education, government relations, and church-state concerns were high in the list. If nothing else, the decisions on "fields" gave the association's leadership some suggestions for priorities. What the convention did not give officers or field secretary was a lot of money to do the job. Nor did it establish any systematic way of obtaining funds—such as dues or assessments. Instead, the financial needs became a prayer priority—not unusual for the many people involved who were supporters of "faith" missions. The executive committee also appointed its hard-nosed businessman, Kenneth Keyes, as finance chairman. He crisscrossed the country with Wright, calling on wealthy evangelical laymen to ask for contributions. Appealing for *them* to help safeguard the free exercise of religion was generally more fruitful, he recalled, than contacting denominational leaders who had trouble funding existing budgets.

Poised for United Action: Participants break from their deliberations in St. Louis during the opening day of the National Conference for United Action Among Evangelicals, April 7, 1942.

Yankee Ingenuity: Rev. and Mrs. J. Elwin Wright, at the end of his five-year tenure as NAE's founding director, 1947. Wright had earlier founded the New England Fellowship, out of which the idea of, and plans for, a national association emerged. Courtesy of the Billy Graham Center.

A Voice for the Unvoiced: Harold John Ockenga, founding president of NAE, in the 1940s. His keynote address in St. Louis set the vision and mood of NAE for decades to come. Courtesy of Park Street Church, Boston.

UNITED EVANGELICAL ACTION

VOL. 1, NO. 1   BULLETIN OF THE NATIONAL ASSOCIATION OF EVANGELICALS FOR UNITED ACTION   AUG. 1, 1942

Trusted Leader At The Helm

Dr. Harold John Ockenga, Boston Pastor, Heads Association

T h e paramount need of evangelicals is for an organization by which their convictions may be expressed and their actions unified. "One shall chase a thousand but two shall chase ten thousand." Totali-

Dr. H. J. Ockenga

tarianism has taught us that we must have a new technique in action or we will be liquidated. We have been speaking, acting and working independently of one another. As a result we have had no means of influencing the great national trends.

Representative Gathering

At St. Louis, from April 7th to 9th, a historic meeting was held. A widespread conviction for the need of such evangelical testimony and action caused the spontaneous response to a call sent forth by a temporary committee for a council of evangelicals. One hundred and forty-seven leaders responded from all parts of America. The conference was marked by a sober realization of our need, and by a new disposition on the part of evangelicals to cooperate with one another. The three days of discussion resulted in a temporary organization.

Dr. Ockenga Drafted

The new association was exceedingly fortunate in being able to draft as its first term president Dr. Harold John Ockenga, the dynamic and youthful pastor of historic Park Street Church of Boston. Dr. Ockenga's unusual ability, both as an administrator and scholarly minister of t h e W o r d, splendidly qualifies him to head this great national movement of evangelicals.

(Turn to page 2)

REGIONAL CONFERENCES SWEEPING COUNTRY

New York and Boston Report Revival Spirit As Initial Conferences Are Launched

RADIO PROBLEMS REVIEWED

By J. Elwin Wright

Radio Institute Meets

The Institute for Education by Radio, held at Columbus, Ohio, annually, has become a clearing house for ideas in the field of educational and religious broadcasting. The Religious Work-Study Group of the conference for 1941 appointed a committee to draft certain recommendations for changes in policy for religious broadcasts. The recommendations, five in number, were submitted to the 1942 conference, held May 3-6. These were as follows:

Conference Recommendations

1. THAT religious radio programs, received in the homes of individuals of different religious faiths, should be addressed to a cross-section of the public — to Protestants, Catholics, Jews and non-believers—and not to members of any one faith. Exceptions to this recommendation are special event religious programs such as denominational conventions, eucharistic C o n gresses and Passover services.

2. THAT religious programs should not attack beliefs of members of other faiths. When religious doctrines are expounded on the air, the presentation should be strictly affirmative.

3. THAT the broadcasting of religious programs should be provided by radio stations in keeping with their responsibility to serve the "public interest, convenience and necessity." Religious programs, like educational broadcasts, should be presented on a sustaining basis, without payment for time.

4. THAT time available be allocated by networks or local station management in cooperation with advisory committees from the various faiths, in order to insure fair treatment of the various religious bodies seeking representation on the air. Also, that time for religion on the air should be provided in accordance with (a) the merit of the program for which time is sought; (b) the numerical strength of the various religious faiths within the service areas of the networks or local stations.

5. THAT regular religious radio programs should not appeal for contributions either directly or indirectly, for the support of the radio program itself. Nor should a charge for sermons, pamphlets or religious objects, distributed through religious programs, be used by the sponsor as a means of raising funds.

Doctrinal Basis of The National Association of Evangelicals For United Action

It shall be required that those holding membership shall subscribe to the following doctrines:

1). That we believe the Bible to be the inspired, the only infallible, authoritative Word of God.

2). That we believe that there is one God, eternally existent in three persons: Father, Son and Holy Spirit.

3). That we believe in the deity of Christ, in His virgin birth, in His sinless life, in His miracles, in His vicarious and atoning death, in His bodily resurrection, in His ascension to the right hand of the Father and in His personal return in power and glory.

4). That because of the exceeding sinfulness of human nature we believe in the absolute necessity of regeneration by the Holy Spirit for salvation.

5). That we believe in the resurrection of both the saved and the lost; they that are sav-

J. Elwin Wright, Chairman Committee on Doctrine

ed unto the resurrection of life and they that are lost unto the resurrection of damnation.

6). That we believe in the spiritual unity of believers in Christ.

RALLIES ATTRACT FINE GROUP OF EVANGELICALS

A New York regional conference, in Calvary Baptist Church, on Monday, June 8th, brought a large and distinguished group of Christian leaders to that city to acquaint them with the N a t i o n a l Association of Evangelicals for United Action, which was formed at St. Louis, Mo., April 7-9, 1942, and to discuss further development. On Tuesday, June 9th, an equally representative group met in Park Street Church, Boston, for the New England regional convention.

President Howard W. Ferrin

At the ten-thirty session Mr. Howard W. Ferrin, President of Providence Bible Institute, brought a very stirring and inspiring message on "The Lost Chord, or The Revival We Need." His text was Revelation 2:4—"Nevertheless I have somewhat against thee, because thou hast left thy first love."

Mr. Ferrin's address was followed by a period of prayer for revival. The spirit of God was in this meeting in a very marked way, and there was a time of true humility and melting before God, with petitions for forgiveness and revival.

President Nathan R. Wood

The afternoon session was opened with a very interesting report brought by Dr. Nathan R. Wood, President of Gordon College of Theology and Missions, under the title of "Coronado," for the convention had met at the Hotel Coronado in St. Louis, Mo., April 7-9, 1942. Dr. Wood, speaking not as an officer of the Association but as an interested observer, said, "We have organized with the purpose of providing a clearing house, a congress, or better yet a united voice, a combined influence of countless evangelical — fundamentally evangelical — Christian churches and organizations. It

(Turn to page 2)

Pressing for Action: First issue of NAE's official periodical, *United Evangelical Action*, August 1, 1942. While some expressed hopes for a daily newspaper on par with the *Christian Science Monitor*, the association settled for a more modest format, published twice a month. Publication frequently was reduced to monthly in 1958 and quarterly in 1968. In 1983, the magazine became a bimonthly.

Brass in the Big Apple: NAE executive committee meets in New York, September 1942. Clockwise from head of table: Harold J. Ockenga (president), J. Elwin Wright (promotional director), R. J. Bateman (first vice-president), John W. Bradbury, J. Alvin Orr, Leslie R. Marston (second vice-president), James T. Rider, William W. Ayer, Alex H. Sauerwein, Ralph T. Davis, H. M. Shuman, H. J. Taylor (treasurer), J. Williston Smith (secretary), and Gertrude D. Clark (office secretary).

Fundamental Challenge: New Jersey fundamentalist Carl McIntire in the 1940s. McIntire appealed to NAE on three occasions to unite with his two cooperative agencies, the American and International Councils of Christian Churches. Although he was a close friend of Harold Ockenga, the two men's respective organizations went separate ways, costing NAE support from some key conservative leaders and institutions. Courtesy of the Bible Presbyterian Church, Collingswood, New Jersey.

Steering NAE to New Heights: Houghton College President Stephen W. Paine in the 1940s. NAE's fourth president (1948-50), Paine exercised clout in Washington, pressed for "cooperation" over "separation," and played a key role in the development of the New International Version of the Bible. Courtesy of Houghton College.

Challenging the First Lady: The State Department conference on international human rights in November 1949 where NAE President Stephen Paine (second from right at table) took issue with the Universal Declaration of Human Rights, whose principal drafter was Eleanor Roosevelt (upper left). Paine contended that the document departed from the U.S. Declaration of Independence by setting forth that rights find their origin in the creature, not the Creator. Courtesy of Stephen W. Paine.

Standing Tall: Clyde W. Taylor, in the early days of his NAE career. Beginning with his appointment to the Washington office in 1944, the Baptist minister was a dominant figure in NAE for three decades.

Rolling Out the Banner: George L. Ford, a Free Methodist minister, promotes NAE during the 1950 Billy Graham Crusade in Portland, Oregon. After becoming NAE's Northwest regional director in 1951, Ford rose through the ranks to become first general director. Courtesy of the Billy Graham Center.

World Evangelical Fellowship in the Making: Representatives from the United States and twelve European countries, including the Evangelical Alliance of Great Britain, gather at Hildenborough Hall, in Kent, England, in 1950. Here the committee was formed that issued a call to the 1951 convention in the Netherlands where the World Evangelical Fellowship was born. J. Elwin Wright, representing NAE, is seated second to the right. Lt. Gen. Sir Arthur Smith, seated in the center, was committee chairman. Courtesy of the Billy Graham Center.

Standing Up Around the World: Representing NAE at the first general council (1953) of the World Evangelical Fellowship in Clarens, Switzerland, were, from left, Philip Hogan, J. Elwin Wright, James DeForest Murch, Albert J. Lindsay, Clyde W. Taylor, Frederick Curtis Fowler, NAE President Paul S. Rees, and Elmo J. Van Halsema. Courtesy of the Billy Graham Center.

Flanked by Generals and a Bishop: NAE's Clyde Taylor (center), with other Protestant and Roman Catholic officials, pose with Air Force brass before a 1957 visit to chaplains on the field in Newfoundland and Greenland. Courtesy of the U.S. Air Force.

7

Mister NAE Goes to Washington

WITH OR WITHOUT MONEY in the bank, Wright charged ahead as NAE's first executive officer. Mail poured in from around the nation. The space available in the office at Park Street Church was too small, so he moved the NAE headquarters into a Tremont Street commercial building. The operations of *United Evangelical Action,* which had commenced publication on August 1, 1942, were also moved to the new location. Wright had one assistant for the periodical's editorial side and one for the business side. In addition, at peak times he employed five secretaries.

The Massachusetts statehouse was just down the street, and Boston was his base as well as the traditional "capital" of all New England, but Wright's new responsibilities were national, not regional. The Chicago convention had indicated that it considered dealing with the federal government important, so Wright set off to Washington to see what he could do on behalf of the formally constituted National Association of Evangelicals.

"We must have an office in Washington," the field secretary reported to his board. He mentioned the need for someone based there to help evangelical candidates for the military chaplaincy, to guide mission boards in their communications with the State Department and foreign governments, to champion the cause of Christian broadcasters with the Federal Communications Commission, to monitor legislation that might affect religious liberty, to assist ministerial and missionary candidates seeking draft deferments—and many other needs.

A Small Office in Washington

Without waiting for appointment of someone to take charge of the Capital City function, Wright rented a small office in the summer of 1943. With temporary staff, it opened in September.

The next May, the field secretary was still trying to get a handle on the work in Washington. From Boston, he wrote Frank Stellenwerck, the acting director. Wright asked for copies of bills in Congress which would interest the NAE constituency. Replying quickly, the Washington representative might have recorded for the first time an indication of the budget restrictions under which the office operated. He wrote, "I find the expense of obtaining copies of the individual bills is far too great to be considered." He then suggested that he be notified when the headquarters staff learned of concern about a particular piece of legislation so that he could try to get the text.

In the same letter the acting director in the capital also gave Wright a taste of dealing with the federal bureaucracy. He said a State Department official "in his rambling way indicated over the phone that he would like to get all the details possible as to the mission boards." The writer indicated to his chief in Boston that he was not sure "that we can in any definite way satisfy" the government official, but he suggested how they might try to do so.

Harold Ockenga, the association president, was mentioned in the letter. He had been in Washington to represent NAE, as his successors over the years often would do. In this case, he met with military chaplaincy officials to pave the way for recognition of evangelicals. Making such appointments and making sure that NAE is represented at critical government meetings has been one of the challenging tasks of the Washington office.

Mister NAE Is Recruited

During those first bumpy months, Wright had his eye on someone with exceptional qualifications for taking over the Washington office permanently. Clyde W. Taylor, a former Christian and Missionary Alliance missionary in South America, was then pastor of a Baptist church in Quincy, Massachusetts, and part-time professor at Gordon College. His experience in Colombia and Peru, where the distinctions between state and church were blurred, gave him keen insight into church-state problems. The international exposure had also given him an understanding of the need for protocol and diplomacy, yet he was straightforward. He was an able speaker. And he was impressive physically, with his above average height putting him head and shoulders above most contemporaries.

Taylor accepted the call from NAE and took over the office in 1944. He was to stay there thirty years. It was usually called the NAE missions office in the early years, but he wore at least four "hats" (often more than one at a time) during those decades. Because of his long tenure, his many contacts, his representation of NAE on many platforms, and his unusual service to many individuals and agencies, he became known as "Mister NAE" or "Mister Evangelical" in Washington and throughout the nation.

The territory was uncharted when he arrived in the nation's capital. There was no precedent for an evangelical ambassador, or lobbyist, or facilitator.

"We had nobody showing us how to do it," Taylor once explained, "so we just used our imagination and saw if it would work."

It did work. It worked for missionaries and their supporting agencies at home. It worked for the nationals with whom the missionaries were connected abroad. It worked for college students considering government careers. It worked for many others mentioned in Wright's proposal for a Washington office and some that even the inventive Wright could not imagine.

Taylor's diligence and his desire to be a good representative of the evangelical cause brought him some odd requests. One amateur insect collector asked to be put in touch with missionaries around the world who might be willing to send exotic specimens. Taylor passed that one on to Wade Coggins, his assistant in the missions office. Coggins sent a courteous reply, declining participation in the project but suggesting the name and address of one mission that might help.

Extra-Governmental Tasks

Still other appeals had nothing at all to do with Washington or the federal government, but they were very serious. Clyde Taylor took them seriously and tried to help—often with great ingenuity. For instance, missionaries with children having mental or other disabilities wrote to see if information could be provided on special education facilities in their home states. One family, needing residential care for a son and unable to persuade the state to accept him, sought Taylor's intervention. Their legal residence was in California when Earl Warren was governor (before his appointment to the Supreme Court). The NAE Washington director had no political pull with Warren. But he knew someone in New York State who knew someone in California. She happened to be the sister of the governor's wife. The New York contact respected Taylor's unselfish interest in the welfare of missionaries and told her sister of the case. The information went directly into the governor's office, where his private secretary took charge. Within weeks, the child was admitted to a new state facility.

"You are a man after my own heart the way you tackle jobs and get them done," the father declared in a letter of appreciation for the unusual service. He then referred to an impending visit by Taylor to fellow members of his mission: "You better be walking the chalk line when you meet my gang because they are expecting to see more than a physical giant."

Access to Other Countries

More often, the Washington director's work had to do with matters affecting the freedom of Christians to exercise their faith—at home or abroad. With World War II still going on when he arrived on the job, Taylor spent much of his time in the capital learning how to help missionaries cope with travel restrictions. Issuance of passports to U.S. citizens was not the routine matter then that it has become in the years since. Applicants were required to give reasons for their travel sometimes, and bureaucrats could put off approval for months. By May 1945, Taylor was able to report that he had handled eighty applications, mostly for Latin American missionaries, and had "not been turned down in a single instance."

Believing that a word of commendation might be helpful to the director in his future relations with the State Department, the missions commission of NAE passed a resolution at the 1945 convention commending the passport division "for its record of assistance to Protestant missions" and expressing gratitude "for the statement that the [State] Department is not discriminating between Protestant and Roman Catholic groups in the issuing of passports for Latin America."

In November of 1945, Taylor reported to the executive committee the news that "China has opened doors, and we secured seven passports to China last week." He had been in Washington just over a year at that time, but he was prepared to help missionaries get into China just weeks after Japan surrendered and left China. The executive told the committee happily, "We put ten on ships for that country this week."

Still another challenge was obtaining visas from host countries. In the years immediately after World War II, before many Third World countries gained their independence, that meant dealing with the colonial powers. The British Union Jack was still flying over much of the world then, so there were frequent trips to the British embassy to get visas for India, Nigeria, Ghana, Kenya, Hong Kong, and fields in the Caribbean and elsewhere. Belgium still had a huge colony called Congo (now Zaire) where many missionaries wanted to go, and it took a personal appeal to the consul to get nearly every application processed. French diplomats had to be approached to obtain visas for Vietnam and much of West Africa.

The Help of an Assistant

As soon as he could train assistants, Taylor turned the visa work over to them. The cases were often difficult, however, and the director would have to intercede to get the necessary action.

Avery Kendall, Taylor's secretary for twenty years and a missionary to Panama before she worked for him, handled visa applications during a part of her time with NAE. As former colonies became independent, Washington's Embassy Row grew rapidly. Miss Kendall has vivid memories of dealing with some of the representatives from those new nations.

"The embassy was one place where they were in the driver's seat," she recalled. "They could be as cocky as they wanted to be. You could do nothing about it except just sit there."

Often, she was away from the office for hours at a time trying to obtain missionary visas. She always took along plenty of reading material to occupy her waiting time, she explained.

Miss Kendall learned from Taylor that she sometimes had to revert to hard-line diplomacy for results. In one of her tough cases she had left passports with visa applications at the Embassy of Zaire, and after several days passed she could still not learn when documents would be ready. Her persistent inquiries finally yielded a clerk's pronouncement that she had not left the passports there.

"I shall have to report to the State Department that these passports were lost, and when they were lost," she replied to the Zairean. That brought a quick, "No, don't!" from the other side of the counter. Within a day the passports were found and the visas were affixed to them.

Her efforts were rewarded when letters from those missionaries arrived after they were on the field. She opened Taylor's mail, and often there was note of appreciation for the service provided by the office. Many of the missionaries also put NAE on the mailing list for their periodic prayer letters to supporters. "We got tons of them," she recalled, and she scanned them all.

Dealing with Various Requests

Letters addressed to Taylor personally went straight to his desk, Miss Kendall said, "even if it was obviously a crackpot letter—and we got quite a few of those." Her boss had one file that he labeled "crackpot" and another "dishonest."

In the days before the formation of associations of missionary agencies and before the Evangelical Council on Financial Accountability, Taylor's office was the only place that most people knew to consult if they had questions about the legitimacy of an enterprise soliciting their support and claiming to be a Christian outreach. The secretary said "a lot of inquiries" asked about the integrity of organizations. Taylor was as zealous to defend the reputation of the legitimate agencies as he was to show the dishonest ones for what they were. He knew the personnel and programs so well that in all the years of answering those inquiries he was taken to task only once for a response, Miss Kendall recalled.

That happened when a national was raising money in the United States for work in his home country. The walking reference library on missions told an inquirer that he had doubts that the national used the money overseas to carry out the program he described on American platforms. The national threatened to sue. The office had no lawyer in house or on retainer, so Taylor sought curbside advice from a lawyer friend. The attorney advised that there appeared to be slim grounds for a successful suit. It was not, in fact, ever filed.

During most of Taylor's tenure, the Washington NAE office was in a building at Fourteenth and G

Streets, about four blocks from the White House. (Initially it was a block down Fourteenth at F Street.)

"He was frugal with his own money and just as careful with NAE's money," Miss Kendall recalled, "so we never spent anything on frills to make the place look nice." Not only was it unpretentious, but in her estimate it was "grubby." Taylor did not intend it to be a showplace, but the secretary remembers a few occasions when he expected a distinguished visitor, such as Billy Graham, and asked her to "neaten everything up to look nice." She would try, but given the basic looks of the place and the collection of materials there, "it wasn't possible."

In the crowded quarters, Miss Kendall's desk was just outside Taylor's door. With his booming voice, Taylor "just bellowed," she recalled, "and I could always hear everything he said on the telephone."

That intraoffice communication probably added to the efficiency of the small operation, making it unnecessary for him to repeat to her the promises he made to the caller to send government forms or publicity materials, or to check into a visa application, or to provide some other service. Perhaps more of a factor in the productivity of the small staff was Taylor's complete confidence in his aides and his loyalty to them.

Gracious Demeanor

"Not once did I know him to chew anyone out," the secretary recalled appreciatively. She was embarrassed once when the top executive of one of the affiliated missions called to complain that a serious error was made in the reproduction of a message he had delivered at an NAE event. Long before the advent of photocopying machines, she had not only typed the stencil but had run off multiple copies on a messy mimeograph machine. The missions leader was outraged that the word "not" was omitted from a key passage dealing with doctrine. A reader taking the passage out of context could conclude that the author of the piece believed the opposite of what he claimed. Taylor heard the whole tirade, accepted responsibility for the error without passing the blame on to any member of the staff and agreed to provide a corrected copy to all those who received the original version. By the time he was off the phone, Miss Kendall knew exactly what had happened and what had to be done next, and she was at the point of tears. She started to apologize, but the boss interrupted, "Sis, it just proves you're a member of the human race."

The way Taylor treated his assistants went a long way in overcoming the disadvantages of meager salaries and unattractive surroundings. He delegated tasks, fully expecting them to be completed on time. Miss Kendall laughed in an interview after her retirement, "He had no idea how long it took to get anything done. He thought we could do anything and everything—which sometimes made things a little difficult."

Not only did Taylor and his team do the difficult. To some observers it appeared that they sometimes did the nearly impossible or almost miraculous— providing American evangelicals with multiplied dollars worth of service for every one that was designated to run the Washington office.

8

A Family of Voices

WITHIN A YEAR of the NAE's constitutional convention in Chicago, Elwin Wright saw an overwhelming outpouring of interest. Believers across the nation wanted to cooperate—on many different issues. They also expected the infant association to start serving them immediately.

New impetus was given to the need for action on the radio issue late in 1943 when the Mutual radio network announced that it would follow the example of its competitors, NBC and CBS, and stop selling time for religious programs. Would individual stations follow also? Something had to be done.

Something also needed to be done in education, in missions, in chaplaincies, and in other fields in which evangelicals wanted to cooperate. What should come first? How were priorities to be set?

Wright's adrenalin was pumping. The man in charge of NAE headquarters in Boston was challenged by multiple opportunities. Having several irons in the fire at once stimulated him. While he was supervising NAE's office he was also still in charge of the New England Fellowship.

Spreading the News

Membership applications poured in, with subscriptions to *United Evangelical Action*. Wright was so excited by the reception of the publication that he went to the 1944 convention with this report: "A year ago I was confident that there was a place in America for a newspaper which would be devoted exclusively to news of interest to evangelicals. I wish to say now that I am more than confident; I am certain that such a newspaper can be a financial success as well as a success from every other standpoint. *United Evangelical Action* is gaining hosts of new friends for itself and for our movement. We have now reached the point where it is to remain a full-sized newspaper or be reduced to tabloid size. I personally am convinced that it should remain a full-sized newspaper but should be published twice a month for a limited time, then once a week.

"If we can secure the proper editorial management, this paper can be made a daily within the next ten years, with a subscription list that will rival that of the *Christian Science Monitor*. Why not? There are millions of evangelicals who would support a clean, up-to-the-minute newspaper, with Christian news as well. Our numbers far exceed the Christian Scientists."

The enthusiastic entrepreneur was way ahead of his time. He realized the value of good communications. He also probably expected a successful paper to be a way of uniting a diverse constituency and increasing support for the fledgling association. With his emphasis on increasing the frequency, he showed his understanding of the perishability of news.

But was news more important than keeping faithful preachers on the radio? Nothing more appears in the records about Wright's dream of a Christian daily newspaper. The young organization had to make choices, and staking a claim to the airwaves seemed to be more important at the time. There was no threat to the right to publish then, but evangelicals were alarmed that they might lose access to radio.

Serving as a Catalyst

How the NAE leadership attacked the broadcasting issue was to set a pattern for handling many other major concerns over the years. It also affected development of the association's structure and its ability to represent the "unvoiced multitudes" on a broader basis.

The answer for that day—and on numerous occasions thereafter—was for NAE to serve as a catalyst. NAE invited 150 evangelical broadcasters to meet in a special session during its 1944 convention in Columbus, Ohio (the same city in which Wright had made his appeal to the radio "clearing house" in 1943). New York preacher William Ward Ayer chaired the session. He recognized Vincent Brushwyler of Muscatine, Iowa, a Baptist minister, who moved that "we form a national association of Gospel broadcasters, to be affiliated with the National Association of Evangelicals." The motion passed unanimously, and National Religious Broadcasters was born. Just how the new entity was to be affiliated with NAE was not spelled out. In his history, James DeForest Murch (who was president of NRB in 1956, when he published *Cooperation Without Compromise*), put it delicately: "The exact place of the NRB in relationship to the NAE was worked out in later conventions."

In effect, what NAE did was to spin off an entity that would make broadcasting its priority. That issue would no longer be NAE's primary concern— even if it did take a benevolent interest.

A Pattern Emerges

NRB took off on its own. The officers elected in Columbus were constituted as an executive committee with broad powers. They called a constitutional convention for September 1944 at Moody Church,

Chicago. They authorized establishment of a Washington office (nothing was said in the action about becoming a part of the NAE office in the Capital City) and the retaining of a Washington counsel. Legally, NRB was set up as a corporation in the State of Delaware.

At the September meeting a constitution and by-laws were adopted and temporary officers were elected. A board with rotating three-year terms was also chosen. Among the directors was the Assemblies of God pastor, Thomas Zimmerman, who was later to be president of both NRB and NAE. Familiar names on the first board included Walter A. Maier of "The Lutheran Hour," Theodore H. Epp of "Back to the Bible," M. R. DeHaan of "Radio Bible Class," and Bob Jones (Sr.), then broadcasting from his college at Cleveland, Tennessee.

Significantly, a code of ethics was adopted at the constitutional convention. It specified that all members were nonprofit organizations whose appeals "for legitimate religious purposes" would be "presented in a dignified Christian manner." The rudimentary code, according to Murch, "became a veritable 'Declaration of Independence' from radio racketeers on the one hand and ecclesiastical boycotters on the other."

In the early years, the NRB officers doubled as NAE's radio commission. In that role, they pursued for the evangelical community the sustaining time on the networks and the stations that it thought it was due as the "fourth force." When acting in the role of NRB, the leadership was primarily concerned with protecting the interests of program producers who bought air slots. (There were also a few station owners and operators in the initial membership.)

NRB's start was just before the beginning of a great growth spurt in the broadcasting industry. After World War II new station licenses were granted in nearly every town. The FM band was added to AM, adding to the number of frequencies available. Then television burst upon the scene. NRB boomed. Dues payments by its members became a source of annual revenue. NRB began to stage its own conventions separate from those of its nominal parent, NAE, and soon became more visible. The connection was NAE's formal approval of board members elected by NRB.

Other Offspring

For evangelicals with other priorities, NAE performed a similar service. The association was the primary meeting place for people with common interests. Often, they were encouraged to take united action for the first time at a seminar at the NAE convention. Details of the spin-off organizations vary. Some never had any official relationship to NAE and do not identify themselves with it. Yet, the association had a catalytic role in pointing to a need and furnishing the umbrella under which the organizers met.

Some of the other functions are barely under the edge of the umbrella while others are closely connected to the parent association. Some have spun off children of their own and then died.

Also created in 1944 was the agency now known as World Relief but first as the War Relief Commission. It has grown far beyond the parent in terms of staff size and income. Formerly a commission, it now has the status of a subsidiary corporation, with all of its stock owned by NAE. Although the worldwide relief and development agency raises its own revenue, its leadership has been careful to identify World Relief as a ministry of NAE.

Also started in 1944 was a commission on industrial chaplaincies. The concept of putting ministers in factories was pushed aggressively by some evangelicals, who cited special stress (and ministry opportunities) related to wartime conditions. The commission was dissolved after a few years, but the idea of chaplain-counselors in businesses caught on outside as well as inside the manufacturing arena.

One of the organizations which began under the NAE umbrella but which was never formally related is the Evangelical Press Association. James DeForest Murch was editor of *United Evangelical Action* when he proposed formation of EPA. He was its first president, but the group decided it was best not to be related to NAE. Still, it adopted NAE's doctrinal statement as its own.

The "church school commission" established in the 1943 constitutional convention evolved into the National Sunday School Association in 1945. In 1947, NAE gave birth to the National Association of Christian Schools to promote day schools under evangelical auspices.

Evangelical Foreign Missions Association

Formally organized in 1945 with affiliate status was the Evangelical Foreign Missions Association, known since 1991 as the Evangelical Fellowship of Mission Agencies. From the beginning, its identification with NAE was strong. NAE's Washington office was its office. NAE's man in Washington, Clyde Taylor, was EFMA's chief executive. But even with EFMA, as with other related organizations, its membership did not mirror the NAE membership. The mission agencies of the Conservative Baptists and of the Christian and Missionary Alliance, for example, were active EFMA members long before the denominations they represent became denominational members of NAE. It was an example of NAE's stance of serving and involving nonmembers. The agency also provided services not only to its supporting missions, and to NAE members who were not affiliated with those missions, but also to individuals not related to either.

EFMA, therefore, had a constituency of its own, somewhat different from that of NAE. The parent body gave it some help at the beginning, but it was expected to pay its own way. It thus developed a support system separate from that of NAE.

That pattern, not unfamiliar to those in many of the member denominations and those supporting the personnel of faith missions, meant that member denominations and organizations also had to choose their priorities in giving. One contribution to NAE would not cover all of the related programs. The donor had to decide whether to give to the missions branch, or the broadcasting branch, or to any of the several other entities—or to NAE itself. With each of the agencies usually having pressing needs—and someone within the denomination related to that agency pushing for more support—it was not unusual for the central administration to be left out when the funds going to NAE were distributed.

Neglecting the Parent Organization

Who would champion the cause of paying a power bill or for office machine maintenance contracts when there is a starving refugee child to be fed or some more dramatic cause to support?

NAE did a service for the broad evangelical community when it created the separate entities to handle priority needs, but it sacrificed possible support for itself and lost a measure of control over its program.

Clyde Taylor was frugal because he had to be. The Washington office was a part of NAE's central administration and not a separate entity that raised funds on its own. The dollars were scarce. During most of his years there, Taylor had an assistant who helped with congressional liaison and who dealt with federal agencies. For many of those years that assistant typed his own letters, as did Taylor's assistant for EFMA work. The lone secretary (for many years) handled Taylor's correspondence and calls as well as being the receptionist.

Describing some critical religious liberty cases in a 1947 report to the board of administration, Taylor informed his supervisors that he was frequently asked if the NAE would help with legal costs in precedent-setting trials.

"Thus far funds have not been available for this purpose and we have not been able to have the voice that we should have in our nation's capital," he said bluntly. "We are endeavoring to do as much as we can with the resources that are available."

Taylor told the board in 1952 of the desirability of having a journalist in the office to round out the team and expand the effectiveness of the operation. Because the secular press took note only when he got involved in a controversial matter (such as one that year dealing with attacks on Italian evangelicals), he explained his concern "that they know us not only for these fights for religious liberty but also for a positive approach to every other matter of evangelical interest in our nation." During most of his thirty years in Washington he did without a staffer with news responsibilities.

9

Forging a Strategy After the War

A s WORLD WAR II WOUND DOWN, appreciation for
NAE picked up. It was poised to harness the
energies of Bible believers and to help bring revival
to the land. Revival was a popular theme at the early
NAE meetings. No one questioned that America and
her churches needed a strong dose of it.

The enthusiasm for the young organization
showed up in improved financial support. At the
November 1945 meeting of the executive committee,
a report showed that 316 congregations had sent
contributions that year, compared to 130 during the
same period the previous year. Finance chairman
Kenneth Keyes plotted the increased giving on a
chart for fellow members of the committee. He cham-

pioned the cause of stationing representatives in all the regions of the country, pointing out that a man already working in the Northwest had tripled income from that area.

Regional Representatives

While the rate of growth in contributions was impressive, the dollar totals were not that significant—even in the dollars of that day. The gifts credited to the Northwest region in the first nine months of 1944 amounted to $2,779. In the same period of 1945, Keyes noted, the total was $6,273. He was interested in more than the short-term revenue, however. Keyes was a convinced advocate of the value of advertising. South Florida's leading real estate agent believed that wise investments in advertising paid off in the long term. He saw NAE regional representatives as such an investment—telling the story of the new association and presenting the challenge while raising money.

The concept was approved, and men were recruited to take on the job of representing NAE in several regions. The results were not uniform. Elwin Wright's New England, for instance, never supported an NAE staffer apart from the regional bodies already operating there, the New England Fellowship and the Evangelistic Association of New England. With urging from the leadership of NAE, the New England Fellowship became the regional chapter of NAE.

Ironically, the region in which Keyes lived and had his primary church contacts, the Southeast, never developed as an NAE region. He offered a substantial personal challenge gift to establish an Atlanta office, but the right man was never found to be the representative.

In contrast, the Upper Midwest and the Northwest supported regional workers generously for the quarter century that the plan was in effect. Conventions were held annually, and regional boards were elected to supervise the program. Among the services offered were seminars on various topics of interest to pastors and lay leaders. Some of the representatives learned to function as counselors and confidants of district denominational workers. They also furnished a sympathetic ear to some lonely pastors.

Where there were active regional organizations, they served as "proving grounds" for future leadership in the national organization. They also helped to host national conventions.

Southern Reservations

One early convention was scheduled for Memphis, home of R. G. Lee, temporary chairman of the St. Louis meeting. Wright thought it was important to "show the flag" of the association in Dixie. The plans fell through, however, and there has never been a convention in the Deep South. A few individual Southern Baptists such as Lee have been interested, but contributors to the Eerdmans *Hand-*

book to Christianity in America noted a suspicion on the part of most Southern Baptists: "They disliked being linked with 'northern' organizations such as NAE." Members of that denomination in those early days also had not come to accept the term "evangelical," considering it some kind of a "Yankee" category.

After the Disney development of Orlando as a tourist destination, NAE held conventions there. Support of the organization in the community was not a strong factor in site selection, however. Nor is the tourism capital of Central Florida considered a part of the Deep South.

The fact that only one convention was held in New England was evidence of a lack of interest in the national association in that region. That 1974 Boston gathering had a poor attendance, according to Paul Toms, successor to Ockenga at Park Street Church and himself an NAE president.

NAE's Role in Evangelism

There was one cause, evangelism, which the early leaders believed that everyone associated with NAE would back. It backfired. An evangelism secretary was hired in 1944, but he came to the 1945 convention in a quandary. Melville G. Hatcher reported: "One group insists that our most important task is to make NAE known. . . . They further insist that the preaching of gospel messages and the giving of Bible studies should be left, in large part, to other occasions. Another group believes that we should take advantage of every opportunity so to preach Christ that souls will be saved and believers edified."

The debate was not over whether evangelism should happen or whether it was needed. Everyone wanted revival, and there was general agreement that evangelism and revival went hand-in-hand. At issue was NAE's role. Should it be a catalyst and encourager, or should the association be a primary agent? Objections to the latter role focused on the issue of whether NAE was usurping the role of the church.

Ecclesiastical statesman Paul Rees chaired the evangelism commission, which proposed something of a compromise at the 1945 meeting. It began: "Your commission for evangelism recommends adherence to an evangelistic policy for NAE that shall be broadly conceived and advisedly administered. This policy must take cognizance of the varieties of approach and technic with which our constituent groups carry on the evangelistic task of the Church of our Lord. We, therefore, do not regard it as our function to conduct evangelistic campaigns as a national association, nor to attempt to set patterns of evangelism, but rather to encourage the spirit and practice of soul winning everywhere and all the time. This, we believe, can be done constructively through the sponsoring of evangelistic conferences or institutes, through advising with church leaders and regional committees, and by alert reporting of soul-winning events in the columns of *United Evangelical Action*."

The panel noted that affiliated local associations "may find it eminently feasible and fruitful to conduct evangelistic series." It added that any NAE people in those communities who "deem it inadvisable" to participate should not be considered disloyal to the national association.

The solution which spelled out an "encourager" role for the national organization but left open a "local option" for affiliated groups was satisfactory to a majority. A significant minority, including some Pentecostals and some Presbyterian-Reformed members, thought the policy needed refinement.

With the association's evangelism stance the major issue, the Christian Reformed Church quit NAE in 1951. (It rejoined in 1988.) The National Association of Free Will Baptists left in 1972, partly over the NAE's involvement in the Key '73 evangelism emphasis.

The executive committee agreed to study the matter again in 1965. Dale Cryderman, who had been one of the youngest delegates in 1943, was chairman of the evangelism and spiritual life commission in 1965 and asked the executive committee for guidance. One question that was settled at that convention was that "the sponsorship of seminars for evangelists for fellowship and inspiration would be satisfactory providing we did not act as a booking agent, as an accrediting association for evangelists, or as an association of evangelists."

While evangelism turned out to be less than a unifying emphasis for NAE, overseas relief won the hearts of the NAE constituency. Newsreel pictures at the end of World War II showed emaciated Europeans. People wanted to help, and this was something that their churches could not do well by themselves. They needed to be a part of a larger organization that would have the ability to work out the logistics and still have some kind of Christian witness in its ministry of mercy.

Cooperation in Relief Work

In its first five years, the war relief agency of NAE received offerings of more than $100,000 per year. Tons of used clothing and other goods were also contributed. Frank Lombar, the commission's director, reported in 1950 that the 1948 cash contributions of $121,871 were multiplied through wholesale purchases, in-kind contributions and other gifts to the extent that $76,000 worth of food and nearly a million dollars worth of clothing (insurance evaluation) were delivered.

The recipients were grateful. He told the convention: "Their letters and other tokens of appreciation coming back to us by the hundreds tell not only of the lives saved from starvation and from exposure beyond physical endurance, but what is far more precious, to a renewed spiritual strength, the revival of a gospel testimony and the saving of a Christian witness that was so nearly lost on the continent of Europe."

Five years after the Allied victory in Europe, Lombar pointed out that there were communities across the continent which still had not recovered: "There are thousands of Christian refugees and displaced persons in Germany with little or no provision for their livelihood. The Protestant ministers and their families in Southern France have barely enough to eat and most of them are wearing the clothing you sent them through your War Relief Commission. . . . In Greece the situation is similar to that of Germany in 1946 and 1947 as the end of the guerrilla warfare left large numbers of our brethren homeless, sick, and utterly destitute."

Opposing a U.S. Envoy to the Vatican

Another post-war situation that united evangelicals was President Harry Truman's 1946 decision to re-appoint Myron C. Taylor as personal envoy to the Vatican. President Franklin D. Roosevelt had sent him to Rome in 1939, but Americans tended to tolerate the appointment when they heard Roosevelt's explanation that such contact was necessary as part of the commander-in-chief's surveillance network in wartime. The envoy returned to the United States soon after Roosevelt's death, and the war ended within weeks.

Protestants who feared that Roman Catholics would try to upgrade the post from "personal envoy" to "ambassador" breathed a sigh of relief when the diplomat appeared to be staying at home. Then Truman shocked his fellow Baptists and other evangelicals when he sent him back in May 1946. The presidential envoy came to Washington in January 1950. He announced confidently that he did not plan to resign, despite some Protestant complaints about his post. Clyde Taylor sent word to regional NAE leaders, and they got churches in the field to send telegrams by the hundreds to the White House, objecting to continuation of the Vatican office. The NAE Commission on Christian Liberty was in session in an expanded meeting that included other Protestant leaders and representatives of the Washington press corps. It dispatched a protest to Truman, questioning the legality, as well as the practical value, of the office. Within two days of his saying he would stay on the job, the envoy resigned. The NAE leaders then sent the president a letter thanking him for accepting the resignation.

That was not the end of the story. Truman tried again in October 1951. He appointed General Mark Clark, World War II hero, as ambassador to the Vatican. NAE with other organizations orchestrated another outpouring of protest to the White House, to Congress, and to the press. By January of 1952 Clark decided it was a job he did not want, and Truman withdrew the nomination.

91

10

Standing Up in the Military

F AR FROM HOME AND CHURCH, Air Force Sergeant
George Stalker was active in the chapel at his
base in Spain. He taught an adult Sunday school
class and invited its members to his home for monthly
meetings. He also ordered Moody Bible Institute
materials on the subject of the family so that he and
other airmen could join in a study of what the Scriptures said on this key topic. His desire to know the
Bible better and to help others on the base do so was
appreciated—except by the base chaplain.

With his commander's backing, the minister in
Air Force blue forced Stalker to stop the unofficial
studies with Moody materials. The regulations were
on the chaplain's side because they specified that

only ordained clergymen could lead on-base religious activities.

The sergeant was not ordained, and he certainly was not commissioned as a chaplain. Case closed? The chaplain might have thought so for a while, but the Christian airman was convinced he was being deprived of a constitutional right to practice his faith.

Word of the injustice in Spain reached Washington soon after Floyd Robertson retired from the Navy and became director of the NAE Commission on Chaplains in 1960. His portfolio included not only helping evangelical ministers get into chaplaincy but also a concern for the spiritual care of evangelicals and others serving in the military. The mild-mannered Robertson took the latter part of the assignment as seriously as the former. Even though he was new in this job, he was not at all intimidated by the prospect of dealing with the armed services bureaucracy. He had completed twenty-two years on active duty, retiring as a lieutenant commander. During his last decade in service he had been an aide to top admirals in Europe—first to one planning the creation of the North Atlantic Treaty Organization (NATO) in Paris and then to another running the NATO Southern Command from Naples.

Bucking the Military

Robertson had joined the Navy as a seaman and was one of those rare sailors known as a "mustang"—one who rose from the ranks of enlisted men to become a member of the officer corps. His appearance and demeanor did not suggest the spirit linked to the wild mustangs of the Western range, but the Air Force case proved otherwise. When he had a mission to accomplish, he went after it. He knew the protocol, and he could deal with the mightiest. It made no difference if they were generals or admirals, colonels or captains, top sergeants or corporal-clerks.

In the case from Spain, it was a general that the new NAE representative went across the river to see at the Pentagon. The Air Force chief of chaplains then was Gen. Robert P. Taylor, one of the revered survivors of the by-then fabled Bataan death march of World War II.

After Robertson outlined the case to him, Taylor responded that he would "fix it" since he now understood that the airman was a responsible Christian.

But the NAE representative was interested in more than a quick fix, and the general was taken aback somewhat by his reply. "Thank you very much, but that is not my basic concern. Did your chaplain rightly interpret your Air Force regulations?"

Standing behind his man, the chief of chaplains indicated that his subordinate in Spain had followed the letter of the law but then he assured Robertson the regulations "don't apply to your people," who "can have Bible studies any time they want to."

Persistent about the principle at stake, the commission director asked the chief to tell him who was covered by the offending rule. Taylor's explanation was that it was to keep out the cults and sects that were becoming more aggressive, and he named the Jehovah's Witnesses as one example.

"I don't want to be misunderstood," Robertson responded, "but if that is the purpose of the regulations, I guess I am here to protest on behalf of the Jehovah's Witnesses. If you, as chief of chaplains, can control *them*, the next chief may elect to control evangelicals."

The NAE staffer didn't get fast action, but he got it eventually. Within two years of his confrontation with the chief of chaplains, the Air Force issued new regulations permitting noncommissioned volunteers to lead religious gatherings on base.

Recalling the case, Robertson said it was a matter of "simply insisting that this is unconstitutional."

Defending Religious Liberty Abroad

Solving the Spain case was one of Robertson's earliest assignments with NAE's Commission on Chaplains, but it was only one of many during three decades in the Washington office. The Navy veteran had a special place in his heart for Christians in military service since he traced his own conversion to Christ to a time when he was in the Navy. The new believer had no "back home church," so he sought Christian nurture and fellowship among other sailors. Sometimes he met with civilian evangelicals when he had shore duty.

One such occasion was during his assignment in Naples in the early 1950s. During that tour of duty, he "enjoyed delightful fellowship" with missionaries to Italy. He learned from them, among other things, that the religious freedom taken for granted in America was not as easy to come by in other nations. The victorious World War II powers required Italy to write religious liberty guarantees into its post-war constitution, but in the decade following the surrender some local authorities were not complying with the new provisions. Getting involved with some of the missionaries, Robertson was able to help the evangelicals get through some legal tangles. At the same time, his own sense of the importance of religious freedom was heightened.

That experience served him well when he went to work for NAE in 1960.

"Again and again and again we found religious freedom being violated," Robertson said. Sometimes it took only a call or a letter to the appropriate officer to get remedial action. Other cases required teaming up with representatives of other organizations to present a solid front to stress the importance of the issue. Occasionally, a well-placed congressman agreed to handle a matter. Sometimes, help was enlisted from outside Washington—such as when a couple of Harvard law students went to court with a "free exercise" case to nail down the right of chaplains to teach their own beliefs. Publicizing certain cases of discrimination brought results.

Clyde Taylor, who had directed the commission intermittently since taking over the NAE Washington office in 1944, had recruited Robertson. They first met by correspondence, when the Navy officer was trying to help some of his missionary friends at Naples. His next tour of duty was at the Pentagon, and during that time he and Taylor became friends. His last assignment for the Navy was at San Diego, and as that tour was ending, Taylor asked him to consider returning to Washington to take over the commission portfolio.

Tactics to Achieve Change

The "mustang" moved into civilian life, but he learned quickly that he could not abandon the spirit accompanying that nickname if he was to get his job done and keep up with Taylor. Increasingly, the senior NAE man in Washington asked Robertson to represent him at some function or otherwise to wear one of his several "hats." The commission staffer also realized that, even though the Commission on Chaplains and the Office of Public Affairs were distinct entities within NAE, their work overlapped, In fact, he noted, it was often "convenient" to upgrade an issue which first came to him as commission director to one handled by the public affairs office. When a policy change was needed, and the Pentagon brass was resistant, Robertson and Taylor would get their heads together to move the matter into a larger forum. Along the way, the Navy veteran was given the additional title of assistant to the secretary of public affairs.

One stubborn case upgraded within the office was of particular concern to evangelicals in the military and to their families and civilian brethren. It concerned the Sunday school curriculum used in chapels on U.S. bases around the world. The materials came from a central source, and they were mandatory. Chaplains did not have the option of ordering more acceptable literature from other publishers. Bible-believing personnel not only found the lessons inadequate, but some violated their convictions.

When attempts to get relief through the chiefs of chaplains of the various services failed, Robertson recalled, "we pushed it up to the Department of Defense level" (above the three branches) "and then to Congress." Taylor embraced the cause. With Robertson as his public affairs assistant, they marched up to Capitol Hill to present the matter of "government established religion" to a key Southern Baptist legislator. Mendel Rivers was a veteran member of Congress from South Carolina who chaired the House Committee on Armed Services. He "took our cue," according to Robertson, and it wasn't long before the Pentagon gave NAE a commitment that the curriculum would not be mandatory.

Balancing Constitutional Concerns

Americans in military service often had no opportunity for participation in organized religious activity except in base chapels. Whether stationed in Germany or the Philippines or at an installation far from population centers in the homeland, they and their dependents relied on chaplains as their "ministers away from home." It was the business of the NAE office to see that the programs they offered, while necessarily without denominational label, were not also "least common denominator" religion. Robertson sought to keep in view both the "free exercise" and the "no establishment" clauses of the Constitution's first amendment. Nixing a required educational curriculum out of the chapels was an example of the latter, while asserting the rights of chaplains to teach their own beliefs was an example of the former.

Evangelical chaplains gained numerically and in stature during Robertson's three decades of stewardship in Washington. When he took the NAE job, only fifty-four chaplains with any kind of NAE connection could be identified. When he retired in 1991, there was a total of more than five hundred—either with direct endorsement by the NAE commission or from a denomination related to NAE but with its own endorsing mechanism.

Some evangelicals believe that there is still a problem getting fair treatment for their chaplains when it comes to promotions and assignments.

Robertson understands their concerns, but he has also seen more and more of the men related to the commission take high positions. That was illustrated in the year of his retirement by two Army colonels. The command chaplain for Operation Desert Storm in the Middle East was Colonel David Peterson, a minister of the Presbyterian Church in America, an NAE member denomination. He had charge of the work of the hundreds of chaplains working in that campaign—chaplains who reported an unusual spiritual interest on the part of the troops.

And when the commission chose Robertson's successor it didn't have to look far from the office. Across the Potomac, Colonel James D. Edgren was a top aide to the Army chief of chaplains at the Pentagon. He is a minister of the Christian and Missionary Alliance, another NAE denomination. Edgren took the commission post upon retirement from the military.

11

The NAE Idea Goes Global

FREEDOM TO EVANGELIZE at home and abroad was one cause that could unite evangelicals, and Clyde Taylor deftly combined his two main jobs in working for religious liberty. As director of NAE's Washington office, he was charged with dealing with the U.S. government as well as with the embassies representing nations around the world. As the Evangelical Foreign Missions Association's executive, he was responsible for opening closed doors for missionaries.

Moreover, his first boss in NAE was the visionary Elwin Wright, already a veteran fighter for religious liberty. Wright had learned lobbying in the legislative halls of New England as well as in town halls and school board offices. He had also taken on Washington and union chief James C. Petrillo in the threat by organized labor to take the "Old Fashioned Revival Hour" off the air.

But among the more interesting responses to Wright's efforts as the first executive of NAE were some from overseas. Believers in other countries wanted to join NAE. Reluctantly, Wright replied that the new organization was a *national* association—not *international*. But even though he didn't receive them as members, he kept their names and addresses for a separate mailing list. One of the main concerns of the applicants from other nations was religious liberty. Some of them said they needed the help of American Christians as they tried to gain the right for certain kinds of witness in their lands.

International Opportunities

Wider areas of evangelical cooperation were also suggested by overseas Christians, and the NAE leaders saw them as a logical extension of their assignments. Some would not be logical, however, unless they were under a truly international umbrella. Wright and Taylor began probing the concept of a world body of which the association in the United States would be a part.

The old Evangelical Alliance in Britain was still active, and there were questions about whether it actually considered itself an international fellowship (given that its official name was "World's Evangelical Alliance"). NAE's first president, Harold Ockenga, undertook a diplomatic mission with T. Christie Innes, another statesman. They went to England in 1946 to sound out Alliance leaders, who gave them a green light about the desirability of a truly global fellowship of evangelicals. Their trip was followed quickly that fall by Wright's visit to Britain, Germany, Belgium, the Netherlands, France, and Switzerland.

The father of the New England Fellowship and the National Association of Evangelicals saw still another level of cooperation developing. He wrote to his supporters, "If the great task of the church—world evangelization—is to be accomplished, those who stand for the gospel of our Lord and Saviour must learn to stand by and for each other." New England, he suggested, is destined "to provide a pattern for the entire world in operative evangelical work." Upon his return home Wright reported that national associations were being formed in each of the countries that he visited and that the next step was "an international congress of evangelicals for the consideration of plans for cooperation across the world."

In the Evangelical Foreign Missions Association office meanwhile, Taylor was realizing new reasons for an international organization. Some of the churches started by missions were maturing with nationals now in charge rather than missionaries. In some, a new generation of leadership was arising.

Many of the former colonies were moving toward independence and the spirit of nationalism was developing. Christian leaders overseas were also being courted by representatives of the World Council of Churches, which was moving toward formal organization before World War II interrupted and then was founded officially in 1948. Some alternative was needed.

An Alternative to the World Council

Taylor and Wright, through their extensive contacts with mission executives, missionaries, and national church leaders, encouraged the formation of national associations of evangelicals and, eventually, of an international organization. A preliminary exploration of the idea of a global fellowship was called for Clarens, Switzerland, in 1948.

Two representatives of the (British) Evangelical Alliance attending the meeting on the shores of the Lake of Geneva cautioned that Europe was still in the early stages of recovery from the war, and its evangelical churches were not ready to take on responsibilities for anything other than their own recovery. But with more lead time, the next consultation was called a "delegate conference" and held in England in March 1950. There, NAE representatives joined the British hosts and evangelicals from eleven European nations. This event, followed by a similar one in Boston six months later, set in motion plans for the "International Convention of Evangelicals" in the Netherlands in August 1951.

As a part of the preparation for what would be the founding convention of the World Evangelical Fellowship, Taylor and Wright were sent on a journey of more than three months to promote evangelical cooperation. They circled the globe and were encouraged to learn that national fellowships were being formed in a number of countries.

By this time, Wright had finally succeeded in getting NAE to relieve him of his duties as the national association's top executive. R. L. Decker, then the president and a Kansas City Baptist pastor, assumed additional duties. When his presidential term ended he became part-time executive director. The offices were moved from Boston to Chicago. Wright became assistant to the president first and then secretary for international cooperation. In 1950, NAE established a commission on international relations, with Ockenga as its chairman and Wright as executive secretary.

Forming the World Evangelical Fellowship

Wright and Taylor were both on the small planning committee which organized the 1951 constitutional convention of WEF. It was held at a student hostel named Woudschoten, near Zeist in the Netherlands. Participants came from twenty-one nations, and the total number of delegates, observers and guests was ninety-one. On the opening Sunday, the morning worship service was led by Frederick Curtis Fowler, then president of NAE. Two days later Fowler made the motion to form the WEF. The new international body framed a doctrinal statement similar to that of NAE, but not a carbon copy. With that basis established, the convention then decided that membership would be open to those who could embrace that expression of historic Christianity. The convention rejected the concept that the global umbrella organization would be open only to those who were members of churches not aligned with other ecumenical bodies. In so doing, it followed the pattern of NAE, and it distanced WEF from those who would make separation from the old-line churches the primary criterion.

Election of Gen. Sir Arthur Smith of England as president linked the new organization with the British Evangelical Alliance. He headed the initial "general committee" which managed the organization's affairs between conventions. The United States was represented on the committee by one minister, Harold Ockenga, and one layman, Massachusetts industrialist John Bolten, who was also designated treasurer.

The principal office was to be in London, where F. Roy Cattell was co-secretary with the main administrative responsibilities. The other co-secretary was Elwin Wright, working out of Boston and charged primarily with starting national fellowships in countries where none existed. A British missionary to India, A. Jack Dain, was to join the staff by year's end for "coordination of missionary interests in Great Britain and international aspects."

A Low-Key Approach

Two international speaking trips were among the early priorities of the new organization. To build support in the United States, a six-week itinerary in the fall of 1951 took the WEF president, Gen. Arthur Smith, and Toronto pastor Oswald Smith around the country. They addressed mass meetings of evangelicals in thirty-seven cities. On the day after Christmas that year, Elwin Wright took off on another world tour in the company of Minneapolis pastor Paul Rees, Fowler's successor as NAE president. Their stops in twenty-four nations were designed to minister to evangelicals, to promote evangelical cooperation and to learn how the worldwide association could serve in those nations.

Rees and Wright's findings were to influence the direction of WEF—and NAE—for years to come. In India, for instance, they found an already functioning (though only a year old) and vibrant Evangelical Fellowship of India. Wright wrote that he believed "it is destined to exercise a great influence on the spiritual life of India." He also noted that the Indian association "is lifting a high standard spiritually, is tolerant and friendly to all groups, and is attaining a great degree of respect among all organizations." India was one of the first countries to attain independence after World War II, and her Evangelical Fellowship set a pattern for indigenous leadership of "national associations of evangelicals" in former colonies. The two visiting Americans realized that it would be harder and harder for new missionaries to enter India in the coming years and that believers would need to rely increasingly on home-grown leadership.

"We are convinced that the best methods of promoting the interests of WEF would be by a concern for the spiritual interests of those with whom we met," Rees and Wright reported, "rather than by direct overtures to them regarding membership."

The emissaries suggested that the low-key approach emphasize the training of national leadership and assistance with literature ministries.

Encouraging a Servant Role for the West

With his reputation as a hard-driving promoter, Wright might have been expected to say more about the role of the missionary in the nations he visited and about how indispensable he considered them to be in organizing national associations or recruiting new members. Instead, after the thirty-one thousand mile tour with Rees, he urged that the older and better financed Western groups assume a servant role in relation to the younger churches. It was not counsel that some American groups wanted to hear, especially those that wanted to call all the shots from their headquarters.

110

Wright was again somewhat ahead of the times. He was deeply impressed with the spirituality of national Christian leaders overseas and convinced that encouragement and fellowship from the West would be more important to them than dictated programs.

WEF moved in the directions suggested by co-secretary Wright and NAE president Rees. A literature commission was one of the first efforts to be established. At the 1953 assembly (the first after adoption of the constitution), Clyde Taylor reported "an imperative . . . for a new strategy which will send forth millions of copies of evangelical Christian literature" for new readers around the world. American missions were getting together on a publication and distribution program, he said, and "we are now well started on the international level."

Emphasis on Leadership Training

Although it got a slow start, WEF's emphasis on leadership training urged by Rees and Wright has turned out to be one of the organization's most durable programs. Originally handled through the evangelism commission (chaired by Harold Ockenga), the theological assistance effort of WEF has assisted in training nationals in a variety of ways. Much of it has been "in-country" work to help future leaders and the seminaries or Bible schools they attend in their homelands. The WEF Theological Commission has also been the catalyst for organizing international accrediting agencies for evangelical institutions. Professors have been stimulated through publications and conferences. Scholarships have been provided to enable some gifted students to study outside their own countries.

When Wright returned home from his first trip as a WEF executive, he set up what he called the "share" program to assist churches in developing countries. He produced a list of projects which donors could adopt to meet a pressing need in a WEF member association. Fresh from his inspection of a number of fledgling schools on his trip, Wright put major emphasis on a drive to send books to fill bare library shelves. He reported to the NAE convention in 1956 that ninety thousand volumes had been provided in response to the call from WEF.

Even though he had determined not to make the push for new members a priority in his overseas contacts, Wright saw the membership virtually double when the 1953 assembly (then called a general council) was held at Clarens, Switzerland. Six more national associations were received formally, as well as others in the "affiliate" category for those that had not yet reached all membership criteria. The hosts for the lake side meeting also dealt with some doubled numbers. They had expected about eighty participants, but 171 registered. Wright had promoted attendance and expected others to handle all the details. Among those attending were fifty-two North Americans who flew to Switzerland on a flight arranged by Wright. This time, twenty-three nations (two more than in 1951) were represented and Australia was the only continent not represented.

The 1953 Clarens assembly re-elected President Smith and Treasurer Bolten and reaffirmed the general directions established two years earlier. Paul Rees was elected a vice-president, replacing Ockenga on the executive committee. By this time, Jack Dain had replaced Roy Cattell in the London office. He and Wright continued as co-secretaries. The assembly decided that it wanted a full-time secretariat with its own office, perhaps in Washington, D.C., but it failed to come up with the financial underpinning necessary for such a shift.

The Dream That Would Not Die

Looking back at the enthusiastic dreamers of Clarens, David Howard as WEF general director wrote in his 1986 history, *The Dream That Would Not Die,* "The plans for a full time executive secretariat were not to be fulfilled for over twenty years. . . . Plans for each member organization to share in the expense of the operation have never fully materialized."

But in the years since those first meetings, WEF has broadened its base so that it now has active participants on all continents and from a much longer list of national associations. It has also been led by distinguished evangelicals from developing nations as well as some from the old "missionary-sending" countries. Among its presidents have been leaders from Asia and Africa. In 1992, when David Howard retires, it is scheduled to install its first general director from a developing country, Agustin ("Jun") Vencer, Jr., of the Philippines.

12

Opening Doors for Missionaries

As a MISSIONARY CANDIDATE in 1952, David Howard personified the intersection of national and international interests at the NAE Washington office. At the end of that summer, with the Korean War going full tilt, Howard had just finished a master's program at Wheaton College and was about halfway to getting the support needed to go to South America with the Latin America Mission.

It was a momentous year for him. He and his wife had become parents of a son that summer, and he also had lost his draft deferment and was reclassified 1A—or most eligible for induction into military service.

The man who would become general director of the World Evangelical Fellowship three decades later appealed to Clyde Taylor, as did many other ministerial and missionary candidates of that era.

"I have no objections to going into the service except that I feel the Lord is leading us out to the field, and I do not care to be delayed in this," Howard explained in his letter to Washington. "The Lord seems to be opening up doors so readily for us that I really feel that He is leading us out to the field at this time."

Taylor replied three days later. He reported to the prospective missionary that he had dispatched his principal assistant for public affairs (then former congressional aide Donald S. McAlpine) to the headquarters of the Selective Service System for a review of his case. The colonel he consulted at the draft office noted that "the law does not mention missionaries, and the local [draft] boards are likely to rely on the strict letter [of the law]." With that in mind, Taylor suggested to Howard the steps that could be taken to satisfy the board as to his eligibility for some classification other than 1A.

Howard followed the counsel. He informed the board of changes in his situation, including his ordination late that year. He became a missionary of Latin America Mission in 1953, beginning a career that eventually led to his position as the top executive of WEF.

While Taylor was deeply involved with the beginnings of WEF at that point, his correspondence with Howard gave no hint of it. He certainly had no idea then that his help to a missionary candidate would be a part of the preparation of the person who would direct the international body at its time of greatest expansion. Taylor's dealings with the federal government, in less than ten years in the capital, had become somewhat routine in matters like draft deferments, visas, and the immigration status of overseas believers coming into the United States.

An Advocate for the Unaffiliated

Many of the requests for help with deferments came from men like Howard, whose schools, churches or missionary societies were independent and not connected with a denomination. Some were studying in nonaccredited schools. A good number of those who contacted the Washington office were eligible for deferment as they prepared for ministerial or missionary service, but they were not sure they were and the Selective Service System personnel with whom they dealt thought they were not. Often it was a case of helping them explain how their unaffiliated churches or missions operated and documenting the steps they had taken which were parallel to those of candidates working in better known bodies. A provision of the law referred to a "regular minister" who was serving a religious organization even though he was not formally ordained, and the draft board members or their staff who were familiar only with large denominations only needed to be shown how the applicants fit the definition of the law.

Working for evangelicals, McAlpine apparently was motivated after learning that the two-year Mormon missionaries routinely received deferments. He wrote to one college administrator seeking help for a student, "If such men can be deferred, surely a man who is giving his life to foreign missions is worthy of the same treatment."

One seminary student expressed his thanks for the help from the NAE Washington office: "The time spent in waiting to hear from the national director of the Selective Service System was a good test of my faith. But it was also a great help to know that your office was doing what they could for me. Now that the answer [reclassification and deferment] has come, my thanks go to our wonderful Lord—and to you, his fellow laborers."

Taylor reported to the NAE board in October 1952 that he had received "a constant stream of appeals for help to prevent the induction of theological students and ministers into the armed services." He noted that providing correct information and some advice on getting their papers in order usually helped solve the problems at the level of the local draft board. Then, regarding cases that had to be taken up with national headquarters, he added, "The miracle is that the headquarters office of Selective Service never seems to resent our constant flow of requests to them for national intervention. Recently we had four cases in one day and yet the top men have called in files, halted inductions, reviewed cases, and in every case where there was the slightest possibility of injustice being done, the service reversed action and granted 4D classification."

Assistance for *All* Evangelicals

Taylor's help was not reserved for members of NAE denominations or others with official NAE connections. The office was there to serve evangelicals, and that's what it did.

One of the most notable examples of helping nonmembers was the 1952 case of persecution of Church of Christ congregations in Italy. The missionaries who planted and nurtured those congregations came from autonomous churches in America which deny that they are a part of any organization and which, in Taylor's board report, were described as holding to a doctrine which opposes denominations. Yet, when they were suffering, the NAE Washington office became the focal point for action. Taylor called together representatives of various organizations working in Italy, coordinated contact with government officials who could exert leverage in the situation, and publicized the plight of the Italian believers.

Another illustration of that unrestricted service was the dilemma of Stan Topple, a medical missionary of the Presbyterian Church U.S. ("Southern").

His denomination was not only *not* a member of NAE, but it was a member of the National Council of Churches. Yet, Topple, an evangelical who worked with lepers in South Korea, turned to "Mr. Evangelical" when he needed help in Washington. While on the field, he had married a Norwegian missionary. Anticipating a furlough in the United States, the couple began the process of seeking an immigrant visa for her. They stopped in Norway on the way to America, but the U.S. embassy in Oslo, which was to issue the permit, refused.

Floyd Robertson of the Washington office was the trouble-shooter in the 1964 Topple case. He discovered that the Oslo consul was digging in his heels because one paper was missing and that the document needed from a third country probably could not be obtained without a bribe. He then went for an alternative, obtaining a statement from a veteran leader of another mission familiar with the Topples' work and their experience in the third country. That "secondary evidence" was then accepted by the State Department, which instructed the embassy in Oslo to grant the visa. Mrs. Topple had permission to go to America within a week of the initial appeal to Taylor.

"The State Department has manifested a genuine interest in this case from the time we first approached them," Robertson wrote, "and to the best of our knowledge they have rendered the maximum cooperation within the limitation of their own rules and regulations."

The tangled immigration situations often arose when an American missionary married a citizen of another country. A Michigan woman was the wife of a Canadian, and her complex problems were the subject of the office's attention on three different occasions over a ten-year period. Before it was all sorted out, an over-zealous consular officer had seized her U.S. passport on grounds that she had renounced her citizenship while living in Canada, obtained a British passport on the strength of her husband's subjection to the Queen, and she lost all of the documents during an uprising in the African country where she served (and where her husband was killed).

One of the happier cases set the stage for a wedding. Harold Lindsell, as vice-president of Fuller Seminary in 1964, asked Taylor to intervene on behalf of a Hong Kong woman who had been denied a tourist visa. The consular office thought she would stay in the United States once she got in as a tourist. Taylor went to bat and wrote directly to the consul in Hong Kong, explaining that she was engaged to a Fuller student who planned to go to the British colony as a missionary after his graduation and after an InterVarsity Christian Fellowship training course that summer. The young man wanted her to visit his colleagues and family in California before they married and left for overseas. Taylor carefully spelled out who would be responsible for her during the weeks she would be in the United States. Within a month (and in time for her to join her fiancé at the training course), the visa was granted.

It often took longer for nationals to receive permission if they wanted to work in America, but the Washington evangelical outpost was persistent. Getting one paperwork tangle untangled took eleven months, but the minister coming to work in a seminary finally received permission through a new immigration bill Taylor had been working on with members of Congress. NAE's efforts paid off again and again as schools obtained professors they wanted, churches obtained pastors, and organizations such as the Billy Graham Evangelistic Association obtained team members from abroad.

Help for Henrietta Mears

One of the most prominent American Christian leaders helped with a personal travel problem was Henrietta Mears, the Christian education pioneer. The popular California author and speaker had an Israeli visa in her passport, and that meant automatic refusal of a visa to enter Jordan in 1952. Her written request to the State Department for a new passport was turned down. The NAE staff agreed to help, walked her passport through the bureaucracy and got the alterations made so that she could then obtain a visa from Jordan. Taylor wrote to Miss Mears, "We are happy that our relations with the passport office are such that they go beyond the necessary to accommodate us." In her letter of thanks she explained, "Being over three thousand miles away, I felt very helpless."

Feeling even more helpless was a Cuban woman married to an American who heard Taylor in a talk at a Christian college. After the speech, the couple talked with the visitor from Washington, who took an interest in the woman's family still in Cuba (in 1961, shortly after Castro's takeover of the island nation). Her sister and brother-in-law had two sons (one approaching school age) that they did not want educated in the communist system. Donald H. Gill, then Taylor's chief assistant for public affairs, discovered newly enacted regulations regarding Cubans. The two little boys got out first to go live with relatives in New York, and they were followed in a few months by the grateful parents.

"Mr. Gill," the sister who initiated the action wrote, "I will never be able to express to you and to Dr. Taylor the gratitude I feel in my heart for Christian men like you. You can be sure that I realize how much of your time and effort you are putting into this, and you can be sure that there is no day that passes in which I don't give thanks to Jesus for your goodness to us."

Breaking New Ground: Participating in the 1961 ceremony for the first NAE office building were, from the left, Robert A. Cook, NAE first vice president; Enoch C. Dyrness, president of the National Association of Christian Schools; Carl A. Gundersen, NAE treasurer and general contractor for the building; George L. Ford, NAE executive director; and Forrest J. Gearhart, vice-president of the Wheaton Ministerial Association.

The "First" Evangelical Center: NAE becomes a property owner as the $100,000, sixty-five hundred square-foot office facility on North Main Place in what is now Carol Stream, Illinois, nears completion in 1962.

Mister NAE: Clyde W. Taylor in his Washington office, 1963. Before becoming NAE's general director in 1964, Taylor held a number of NAE jobs including director of public affairs, director of the chaplains commission, and director of the Evangelical Foreign Missions Association.

Meet the Press: General Director Clyde Taylor fields questions from the media on the major issues of the day at the 1965 NAE convention in Minneapolis.

A Silver Anniversary Tribute: Second Vice-president Hudson T. Armerding (at lectern) honors seven of the eleven past presidents at NAE's twenty-fifth convention banquet, in Los Angeles, 1967. Standing from left are Jared F. Gerig (1964-66), Paul S. Rees (1952-54), Robert A. Cook (1962-64), Leslie R. Marston (1944-46), Thomas F. Zimmerman (1960-62), Harold J. Ockenga (1942-44), Paul P. Petticord (1956-58), and Henry H. Savage (1954-56). NAE president at the time, Rufus Jones, is seated at the far right.

Three Productive Decades: Lt. Cmdr. Floyd Robertson (retired), who directed NAE's Commission on Chaplains from 1960-78 and from 1981-91, in 1968. During his tenure, the number of NAE-related chaplains grew from fifty-four to more than five hundred.

In for the Long Haul: First Vice-president Arnold Olson (left) welcomes Billy A. Melvin, newly elected executive director, at the 1967 convention in Los Angeles. Leaving a post with the National Association of Free Will Baptists in Nashville, Tennessee, Melvin would become NAE's longest serving executive director.

The Coach and His Team: General Director Clyde Taylor with the NAE team in the Wheaton office, 1968. Left to right: Joseph A. Ryan, Southwest regional director; Wilmer N. Brown, Pacific regional director; Donald W. Larson, Upper Midwest and West Central regional director; Billy A. Melvin, executive director; Sherwood Becker, Eastern and New England regional director; Charles J. Anderson, Midwest and East Central regional director.

The Second Ground-breaking: Executive Director Billy A. Melvin, former General Director Clyde W. Taylor, and NAE President Carl H. Lundquist turn the spade for a new and expanded office complex, 1978.

A Rising Structure: NAE staff gather around a sign in front of the under-construction Evangelical Center, 1978.

The Evangelical Center: NAE operations move down the block to a twenty-four thousand square-foot, $836,000 office complex on Gundersen Drive in Carol Stream, Illinois, in 1979.

The Ecclesiastical Diplomat: Executive Director Billy A. Melvin (left) receives first denominational contribution from B. Edgar Johnson, general secretary of the Church of the Nazarene, at 1984 Columbus, Ohio, convention when the largest Holiness denomination was received into NAE. From 1981 to 1990, Melvin persuaded fifteen new denominations to join NAE, resulting in a 74 percent growth in communicant membership of denominations in the NAE family. The Church of the Nazarene was the largest denomination to join NAE since the Assemblies of God joined in 1943.

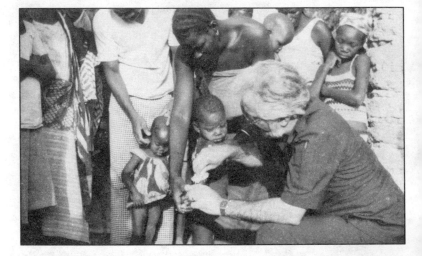

Global Compassion: World Relief Executive Director Jerry Ballard delivers medical care to a child in Burkina Faso, West Africa, 1985. Under Ballard's thirteen years of leadership, NAE's relief and humanitarian assistance arm grew from a limited, $2 million operation to a $20 million full-service relief agency, with a presence in twenty-eight nations.

Public Witness, Public Influence: NAE Public Affairs Director Robert P. Dugan, Jr., testifies before the Senate Judiciary Committee concerning President Reagan's proposed constitutional amendment on school prayer in 1982. After his appointment to NAE in 1978, the Conservative Baptist minister and former congressional candidate coordinated a major expansion of NAE's Office of Public Affairs.

The "Evil Empire" Speech: NAE experienced new levels of public visibility as President Ronald Reagan addressed the 1983 convention in Orlando, Florida. The first of two NAE convention appearances, Reagan delivered one of his most famous speeches, referring to the Soviet Communist system as "the focus of evil in the modern world."

Capitol Exposure: Participants in NAE's Washington Insight Briefing, held every two years to sensitize evangelical Christians to issues of public life, gather on the steps of the U.S. Capitol during the 1986 seminar. A student version of the week-long briefing, the NAE Federal Seminar, has been held annually since 1957.

13

New Vistas of Influence

IN ITS EARLY DAYS, NAE was not bashful, and it learned not only how to take on the bureaucracy of Washington, D.C., but there were times when it seemed to be taking on the whole world. Through its fourth president, Stephen W. Paine (1948-50) the association took issue with Eleanor Roosevelt, U. S. delegate to the United Nations and widow of the country's longest-serving president. She was a principal drafter of the Universal Declaration of Human Rights and the keynote speaker at a State Department-sponsored conference on international human rights in November 1949. Paine, president of Houghton College, was a delegate to that Washington conference.

Mrs. Roosevelt, herself an American institution by this time—four years after her husband's death—came to the conference to advocate adoption of a covenant of political and civil rights extracted from the U.N. declaration. A companion document incorporating social and economic rights was seen by the former first lady as too radical to stand a chance of acceptance until governments became more liberal.

About 125 organizations were represented, and the general response to the keynote address was supportive. In fact, after Mrs. Roosevelt sat down, one representative of the labor movement and one from the Unitarian Church took the floor to praise her but also to suggest that she should have gone further. They wanted to go ahead with the social and economic elements in the proposed covenant. It was beginning to look like a steamroller.

Fearing that the State Department would believe everyone was of the same view, the impressive Paine sought recognition.

Inverted Truth

Not only did the scholarly NAE president criticize the social and economic proposals as socialistic, but he struck at the very foundations of the Roosevelt-drafted declaration.

"It begins with the assertion that man has a certain 'inherent dignity and inalienable rights,'" he noted. "We believe this is an erroneous point of beginning. The founders of our nation started, not

126

with certain rights inherent in man, but described man's rights as given by God, saying that man is endowed by the Creator with certain inalienable rights. . . . Our forefathers went on from man's divinely-given rights to the premise that governments get their rights from the people, from the consent of the governed.

"The Universal Declaration goes on from its start and sets forth a situation where the individual apparently owes his rights to the grant of the government. . . . the Declaration sets the United Nations above the rights of the individual and implies that those rights originate with the UN and are maintained by its sufferance. Our constituency of evangelical church people would, I am sure, deem this an inversion of the correct viewpoint—the one held by the early leaders of our nation."

Paine then pointed to specific provisions in the economic and social sections which he believed to be objectionable to Americans. While his intervention didn't bring the conference to its feet in tumultuous applause, he gave heart to at least one other person there, the Mormon representative. He, in effect, told the other delegates that he was in substantial agreement with the NAE representative. A State Department official closed the day with a strong suggestion that delegates push for only what was obtainable.

In his *Cooperation Without Compromise* in 1956, James DeForest Murch observed that "Dr. Paine's view is now widely accepted by a very considerable sector of American Christianity" and that without his statement "there would have been no open stand for the orthodox Christian viewpoint" at the conference. Murch went on to suggest that the NAE president's 1949 challenge was even a "decided factor in the reluctance of Congress" to move on the U.N. declaration and its covenant.

McIntire's Final Appeal

NAE also turned to Paine to build its main case on another international front. Carl McIntire had organized the International Council of Christian Churches (ICCC) as a protest against the World Council of Churches, just as his American Council of Christian Churches was intended to counter the Federal (later National) Council of Churches. When McIntire learned of NAE plans to help start the World Evangelical Fellowship, he urged NAE to drop those plans and join his international body.

"If you proceed," he wrote, "we believe a grave responsibility will rest upon you to explain to the whole world and the Christian public why you must do it."

Then the fiery separatist closed with this appeal: "We need you, your help, and strength. We want you. We love you in the Lord. God did a mighty work in [the ICCC organizational meeting at] Amsterdam. It far exceeded what we thought or asked. But now He is opening doors of service and testimony beyond anything we have dreamed. We must face this thing. Please, brethren, come with us."

Paine, as NAE president, responded to the "fine letter," promising that the April 1949 meeting of the board would give "prayerful and careful consideration" to the invitation to join the International Council. He then asked McIntire if his council would "accept all of the members of NAE should these be willing to join." Asking for an early reply, he then closed with an appeal for prayer "that the Lord will make us all humble enough to forget any past unpleasantness and look upon each other as brethren in the Lord, willing to work together for His glory."

McIntire, who carried on much of his communication with other groups through his periodical, the *Christian Beacon*, dropped the subject. He often printed full texts of documents from "the other side," but the Paine letter asking about acceptance of NAE members never appeared. The NAE president knew that the answer would have to be negative unless the ICCC founder suddenly changed course and repudiated his doctrine of separation from bodies that he judged heretical.

"We notice from church history," Paine said in his NAE presidential address in 1949, "that wherever a body arrogates to itself the role of the one true church, persecution and pressure and coercion will follow, given the occasion." In much of the message he compared the organization and methods of the International Council and the Federal Council with those of

NAE, always using courtesy in his references to the others.

The Wesleyan Methodist college president told the convention that there were millions of American evangelicals who would be ineligible for membership in McIntire's councils. Therefore, he concluded, "if evangelicals are rallied to the witness of the faith, it will have to be under a banner such as we of NAE have humbly and under God been endeavoring to raise to His glory."

The Problem of 'Separation'

That convention speech, published in expanded form in 1951 as *"Separation"—Is Separating Evangelicals,* showed how numerous attempts had been made to avoid duplicate organizations and how McIntire's forces had blocked them.

Paine also demonstrated how the American Council had not been consistent with its own principles in a variety of situations. He concluded, however, that if the interpretation of separation were followed consistently, "there would be no city-wide evangelistic campaigns" or other such endeavors.

"While we will grant that in evangelical circles, yes within NAE, there will be found varying appraisals of city-wide evangelistic campaigns, yet few if any evangelicals outside the American Council would say that this type of evangelism should be abandoned if it cannot be carried on within the framework of absolute 'separation,' which the above article [in the *Beacon*] apparently admits is the case," Paine wrote.

Claiming support in Scripture (Romans 15:7), Paine proposed an alternative approach. He said "the unifying principle which is needed in Bible-believing interdenominational life is that of extending untrammeled evangelical fellowship to all Bible-believing Christians as such, uniting them in a witness to the historic Christian faith and maintaining a clear witness against apostasy."

A New Bible Translation

The evangelical college president demonstrated his kind of cooperation in still another major effort that was to have global effect much later. The NAE education commission, of which he had been an active part since its beginning, named Paine to a committee to consider the need for a new Bible translation. The Christian Reformed Church (not then a member of NAE) was moving along a parallel path. The study committees from both NAE and the CRC got together in Grand Rapids in 1961 and decided to cooperate in calling a wider group to study the feasibility of a new translation.

One meeting led to another, and in 1966 Paine was elected chairman of the Committee on Bible Translation, which was not connected organically to either of the originating organizations. By the end of 1967 the International Bible Society (then New York Bible Society) became the official sponsor of the project, with the veteran NAE leader and educator continuing as chairman. The decision of the society's board, he recorded in his diary, was an "epochal thing."

Paine and Edwin Palmer, who was hired as executive secretary of the committee, molded the team of translators that would produce the New International Version in 1978. The chairman's daughter, Miriam P. Lemcio, wrote in her father's 1987 biography, *Deo Volente,* that the scholars working on the NIV were "a unique blend of individuals, like a large, loving family where differences of opinion are ultimately less significant than a common heritage."

With the team members sharing Paine's vision, they were working not just for a version to replace the King James Bible, still popular with evangelicals. Nor were they aiming only at an American audience. The new Bible was to be for the whole English-speaking world, and specialists from five nations were recruited to help with the translation. It was an international effort. And its purpose was to produce a version that would be useful. In the words of the original proposal from a Christian Reformed congregation, the new translation should "make God's Word easier for our children to understand" and should "make the Word more readily understandable to those unfamiliar with it as they are confronted with it in missionary and personal work."

It succeeded far beyond anything imagined by any of the translators or sponsors. On the tenth anniversary of publication (1988), distribution had surpassed fifty million copies—not insignificant for a project that had some of its origins in a small NAE committee.

14

Trials and Tribulations

WITH MANY OF ITS MEMBER congregations—as with American religion in general—the National Association of Evangelicals enjoyed a time of relative acceptance and success in the 1950s. NAE's stature grew in Washington particularly, with NAE gaining a reputation for defending persecuted Christians in numerous hot spots. It also basked in the glow of its record of delivering relief goods in the years after World War II to millions of war victims and of re-settling thousands of displaced persons from Europe. It was the time of the ascendancy of Billy Graham as a national figure, and his evangelistic crusades were often promoted by the same people as those active in NAE activities. He easily identified with NAE. He also developed a personal relationship with President Dwight D. Eisenhower, who was the first president to welcome an NAE delegation to the White House (in 1953).

Getting through the 1950s was not easy for the young organization, however. There had never been anything quite like this era before on the American scene, and it was blazing a trail. During NAE's first decade, it had run on a lot of enthusiasm and on the leadership of Elwin Wright, who managed to do the job with a lot of his own energy and with only sporadic pay from NAE.

Most of the obstacles that the association faced in those early years were financial. The member denominations, all small, made contributions that were more moral and spiritual than monetary. Some congregations gave funds. Volunteer fund-raisers knocked on the doors of potential donors as crises arose.

A New Executive Director

Wright's transfer to the international scene left NAE without a top executive. R. L. Decker, the Kansas City pastor who was then president, was asked to finish his term as "executive president," spending some time each month away from his congregation to supervise NAE's Chicago office and to tend to other matters for the association. For a while after his presidency ended he was "acting executive director," and finally in 1951 he became executive director. (Harold Ockenga, meanwhile, had turned down an offer to become the top staffer.) Decker never quite made the transition from pastor to administrator, however. After his departure, the executive committee decided to bring in one of the regional directors, George L. Ford, a Free Methodist who had done a good job developing NAE support in the Northwest. It was to be a trial at first. He started in 1954 with the title "associate executive director," and two years later "associate" was dropped. He served until 1964 in the top staff job (and continued active in the association for years after that).

Ford did as he was expected to do. He strengthened the regional organizations and looked to them to introduce new friends to the national association. A "charter plan" was implemented, in which the regional offices signed up new members and kept a designated portion of the dues. It worked well in some areas. But some of the regions had programs of their own, and certain members of the national board began to suggest that the "little NAEs" were taking the concept too far. The membership base expanded somewhat, but the national treasury gained little. Furthermore, some of the regional offices still had to be subsidized from Chicago.

A Catholic in the White House

A new national issue riveted attention on Washington as the 1950s turned to the 1960s. The Democrats nominated John F. Kennedy, the attractive young Roman Catholic senator from Massachusetts, as their presidential candidate. NAE was a tax-exempt organization and was supposed to be nonpartisan, but few evangelicals looked favorably on the prospect of a Catholic in the White House. Whether the candidate would be free of ecclesiastical control if he won the presidency became an issue in the campaign. Many leading Protestants believed he would not be—including quite a few who would not consider themselves conservative theologically. Kennedy's supporters sought to put the issue to rest with his famous speech to Baptist pastors in Houston.

It fell to Don Gill, assistant to Clyde Taylor in the NAE Washington office, to keep the issue alive. He could not do it as an NAE staffer, though, so he took leave of absence to become executive secretary of Citizens for Religious Freedom. He suggested the separate organization as a way to "pull off the fire" of criticism from NAE. It was also a way to get many other Americans involved in discussion of the issue. One of them was famed New York pastor Norman Vincent Peale, known more for his "positive thinking" concepts than for other interests. He chaired a meeting of national religious leaders which Gill set up September 7 in Washington.

Another was Daniel Poling, revered leader of the Christian Endeavor movement and editor of *Christian Herald*. The possibility of Peale being negative on anything—especially on this presidential candidate—whetted the appetites of many reporters, and the coverage of the issue was extensive. He became the focus of the media attention. Gill wrote in his "Capital Commentary" column in the October issue of *United Evangelical Action* that "it became clear that hostile elements in the press had decided upon Dr. Peale as the scapegoat." Later in the campaign, Peale withdrew his opposition to a Catholic chief executive.

George Ford, the NAE executive, said in an interview published in the December issue of the magazine that evangelicals had lessons to learn from the media handling of the religious issue in the campaign. "They found themselves almost totally incapable of dealing fairly and objectively with any Protestant story," he declared. Clyde Taylor agreed: "We were absolutely unable to convince the press that the Protestant concern was the continued separation of church and state and that we were not entering politics nor attacking a person."

In the 1960 post-election article, the two top staffers of NAE suggested that evangelicals establish a priority of better telling of the evangelical story in the media—a goal frequently stated over the years but never followed up consistently.

Concern for All Areas of Life

Taylor, who by this time had been the evangelicals' man in Washington more than fifteen years, made another observation of even broader import:

"The Catholic Church has taught all along that it is interested in every aspect of society, as well as in spiritual matters. Consequently, they get into government and take an interest in every matter of welfare, education, labor, science, etc." He then pointed out that liberal Protestantism had largely abdicated the role of applying biblical truth to all areas of life. He also admitted that evangelicals "have the theology but we have neglected to apply it to these areas of practical concern."

One area in which NAE tried to help its constituency apply their beliefs was communism. Major thrusts were designed to teach about the nature of the communist system as an all-encompassing "religion." A series of articles ran in the NAE magazine. There was also a question and answer column by former communists. One of them, John Noble, was the featured speaker at a series of NAE sponsored rallies around the country.

Even this attempt at educating the evangelical family raised questions about the community's effectiveness in the larger society. After the 1960 election, Don Gill wrote in his magazine column that he had learned in visits around the nation that "evangelicals are much better at talking over the issues among themselves than they are at precinct activities." This, he added, results in a closed circle of influence, and "to break this closed circuit of evangelical influence is the challenge of our times."

The victory of the Catholic candidate represented a severe threat to many evangelicals, who had considered Kennedy's election unthinkable. So many were worried about the immediate impact that Gill took some space in his column to remind readers of the new president's "repeated, forthright commitments to the principle of church-state separation."

Those who received issues of the December issue of *United Evangelical Action* that year might have been either shocked or comforted when they saw page 3 devoted to an urgent announcement, "No Threat to NAE Tax Exemption." The brief article in bold type reported that, contrary to some stories in circulation, NAE was not under investigation by the Internal Revenue Service. It added, "Furthermore, we have just been advised on good authority that the IRS will not revoke the tax-exempt status of any of the many legitimate religious or other nonprofit organizations for statements on 'the religious issue.'" This, the unsigned announcement declared, was a "victory for the freedom of speech and the freedom of religion."

Turbulent Times

Victory or no victory, the early 1960s were for evangelicals a time of increased vigilance but also a time of licking wounds and introspection. Within the NAE leadership, it was a troubled period. A reorganization of the staff was ordered, and George Ford was elevated to the new top job of general director in

April 1963. By September, he had submitted his resignation, explaining that he might have been the Moses needed to lead NAE out of Egypt, but he was not convinced he was the Joshua to claim the promised land. Ford had brought W. Stanley Mooneyham from the Free Will Baptist denomination to be his director of information, and some saw him as heir apparent. The gifted Mooneyham was asked to provide interim leadership in the headquarters, then in the Chicago suburb of Wheaton, but he acted in that capacity only a few months before leaving for an assignment with the Billy Graham Evangelistic Association.

The board turned to Clyde Taylor as a symbol of stability and continuity. He became the general director, with instructions to stay in Washington and only to commute to Wheaton about once a month to supervise the staff there. The man in charge at Wheaton would be called the executive director and would report to Taylor. Chosen to fill that slot was Arthur Climenhaga, president of Messiah College in Pennsylvania, a bishop of the Brethren in Christ denomination, and a former missionary to Africa.

It was a turbulent time without as well as within. Demonstrations for civil rights divided the nation. The assassinations of President Kennedy and later his brother Robert and Martin Luther King, Jr., sparked more disturbances. The troop buildup in Vietnam emboldened anti-war activists. Vatican Council II met in Rome and, as an NAE resolution later observed, altered the posture if not the doctrine of the Roman Catholic Church.

If the 1950s had been a time to join the church, the sixties were a time for wholesale departures. Edward E. Plowman (whose San Francisco church joined NAE in 1965) became known as the historian of the Jesus Generation, and he told an NAE convention a quarter century later that young people left the churches by the millions in the sixties.

Another segment of the population, black evangelicals, left NAE at least symbolically. Attempts had been made over the years to involve blacks in the association, but few participated on a regular basis. During the tensions of the 1960s a separate organization was formed, the National Negro Evangelical Association (now known as the National Black Evangelical Association). One view was that it was another constructive NAE spinoff. Other blacks who had been active in NAE continued, saying that those who started the new group had never been a part of the older body. Officers of NAE, however, attempted to maintain contact with the new organization, and fraternal greetings were exchanged at conventions.

The Climenhaga administration at the NAE Wheaton office lasted three years, with the twenty-fifth anniversary convention in 1967 expressing appreciation for his service at a critical period. The next executive director, introduced at the 1967 convention, was Billy A. Melvin, who had been serving on the executive committee. The executive from the

Free Will Baptist denomination was to become the longest-serving executive director of the association. Melvin instituted streamlining of the field service department to take the association into the 1970s.

15

Relief for a Hurting World

A S DIVISIVE AS UNITED STATES involvement in Vietnam was, the undeclared war in Southeast Asia furnished NAE a field for unprecedented united action. Most of the Protestant missionaries who had worked in Vietnam were evangelicals. The main national (non-Catholic) denomination was evangelical. As the war heated up and multitudes of civilians were put in harm's way, it was natural that calls for help should go out to fellow believers.

World Relief, the NAE relief and development arm, heard the call and responded as it never had before. Organized as the "war relief" commission at the 1944 NAE convention, the agency had expanded its sphere of activity many times since shipping those first bales of used clothing to the European victims of Hitler's expansionism. Koreans left destitute by the 1950s war on their peninsula were the beneficiaries of World Relief aid, as were people shoved around by civil strife elsewhere in Asia and in Africa, those left homeless by typhoons and hurricanes, those hungry and without means of a livelihood because of droughts, those displaced by earthquakes and other disasters, and those in peril because of epidemics or the loss of good water sources.

In all of its projects, World Relief made a name for itself as a distinctive provider. "Food for the body and food for the soul" was a popular motto. It insisted on providing spiritual help along with material aid. Gospel tracts went along with the first clothes sent to Europe.

One reason World Relief could provide the Word of God with physical assistance was that from the beginning it made its distribution of goods through missionaries or national church workers. The first partner agency at the end of World War II was the Belgian Gospel Mission. By sending its help through such experienced partners in the field, World Relief also complied a remarkable record of keeping down overhead costs. Donor confidence soared as financial report after financial report showed how much of the contributed dollar went to help the needy. In some of the early years more than ninety cents of each dollar was spent for food, medical supplies, and other commodities to be distributed on the field.

Vietnam was spotted as a target for special attention in one of Elwin Wright's first trips to Asia for the World Evangelical Fellowship. After a later visit, in 1959, Clyde Taylor pointed out the uniqueness of the situation and the "tremendous promise" for evangelical work there.

The Vietnam Challenge

Only the French, losing a colony in the 1950s, paid much attention to Vietnam in those days. But by the 1960s, Americans began to take note. Not only were increasing numbers of United States military personnel going to Southeast Asia, but the missionaries were alerting the evangelical community to the distress of the people whose lives were disrupted by years of conflict. World Relief began to move in as the kinds of work that could be done were made known.

Tribes of mountain people had been displaced from not only their homes but also from their traditional means of livelihood. High in their catalog of needs was vocational training. Injured and sick children required medical care. Hunger was a fact of life in many villages cut off from their normal supplies by the war. In some of the cities, youth roamed the streets in search of something to guide them.

Relying on the expertise and linguistic ability of the missionaries—especially those of the Christian and Missionary Alliance—World Relief established a variety of aid programs. It also had the often-unexpected help of many American military personnel. The multiplicity of needs and projects to meet them also meant that the agency could recruit staff and volunteers from many backgrounds in the United States. Thus, members of the traditional "peace churches" such as the evangelical Quakers and Mennonites could serve through World Relief in Vietnam along with those who espoused the just war theory.

It might not have been a popular war, but the NAE constituency got behind its overseas aid people to help the victims. Agricultural workers, teachers, doctors, secretaries, and volunteers with other skills served under the World Relief banner. By late 1972, the agency said that it was housing and caring for one hundred thousand of the country's seven hundred fifty thousand refugees. After Da Nang (a city just below the 1954 line dividing North and South Vietnam) was the scene of pitched battle, students from a World Relief carpentry school moved in to begin rebuilding.

The project that may be best remembered by many who prayed and gave in those days is the Hoa Khanh Children's Hospital in Da Nang. It was built by U.S. Marine and Navy volunteers. The secretary of the Navy, on behalf of those units that had initially operated the 120 bed facility, came to the hospital to turn it over to World Relief. A doctor, upon discharge from the Army in Okinawa, took over as civilian medical director at Hoa Khanh. The

148

facility was an obligatory stop on the inspection trips of denominational officials and other NAE personnel. Chief Nurse "Gwen" (Mrs. Nguyen Thi Khang) came to symbolize a hard-working staff of nationals. She was one of the last evacuees before U.S. troops left the country. The agency was forced to close the institution in March 1975 after operating it for five years and treating some one hundred twenty-five thousand in- and out-patients.

The Boat People

Vivid accounts of orphans being evacuated from Vietnam just before the end of the war were followed just after America's withdrawal by even more gripping stories of the first "boat people"—desperate Vietnamese who fled the county in any kind of craft they could find. Those who survived to get to refugee camps in Thailand, Hong Kong, and the Philippines found World Relief workers there to help prepare them for the next phase of their lives. A variety of services was provided in Christ's name, but most important to those looking for a new homeland were English language courses and processing for immigration to North America.

Thousands of churches volunteered to World Relief to sponsor resettlement of the refugee families. For many members of those churches, helping the "boat people" with housing, job hunting, language training, and acclimatization to living in a new place brought the ministry of World Relief down to a very personal level.

Not all of the aid organization's programs were so massive. Jerry Ballard, who was the agency's chief executive officer during the period of its greatest expansion (1978-1991) pointed to one $2,500 expenditure as perhaps the "best money we ever spent." It went to a small clinic in Haiti. The infant mortality rate in that area near Port-au-Prince was reaching 80 percent. Most of the children were dying of infections that began when their umbilical cords were tied off, Ballard explained. The grant from World Relief was used to teach simple hygiene (such as washing their hands and using clean instruments) to midwives, clinic workers, and mothers. The mortality rate decreased dramatically.

Encouraging Chinese Believers

Another small effort close to Ballard's heart was in mainland China. Physicians, who, after many years in prison, were "retired" to villages outside Beijing, established small clinics. "Old folks outside the system" (such as elderly pastors and "Bible women") were served by the doctors, many of whom had become Christians in their student days. They had little medicine or equipment, and World Relief supplied such basics as aspirin and simple bandages. Most important, the agency director suggested, was the encouragement provided to the Chinese believers through that minimal financial investment.

Most of the projects were much larger. Annual expenditures by the time Ballard left were in the $20 million range. They were less than $2 million when he took over. In his last year, World Relief worked in twenty-eight nations.

Increasingly under Ballard's leadership the agency was a multiplier of the contributions from evangelicals. In his report for fiscal 1988 he told supporters that their gifts of $4.85 million produced a total aid package of $19.63 million. "Every dollar contributed to World Relief delivered $4.10 to needy areas of the world," the financial summary stated.

Stretching Dollars

The funds provided by donors were multiplied in several ways. One of the most frequently used methods was to pay only for the shipment of food provided free by the U.S. government. Another was to match aid grants from federal agencies, the United Nations or other organizations. The types of match varied, but sometimes more than five dollars was available from the grantor for each dollar from World Relief.

Because of its "food for the body *and* food for the soul" policy, World Relief could not accept every grant it was offered. Ballard recalled one famine area where the United States foreign aid officials wanted to help feed the victims, as did the NAE agency. However, the country was "closed" in terms of missionary activity, and virtually no Christian workers had been able to move there. No church

151

operated openly. World Relief could have sent in personnel to distribute food, but they would not have been permitted to evangelize or hand out Christian literature, so a $2 million grant was declined.

The agency's chief for thirteen years considered his greatest contribution to be his insistence on working through the church. The concept was "in germ form" when he took over, he said, but under his administration it developed into a methodology. In the organization's early days, missionaries often were the vehicle for delivery of materials and services. By Ballard's time, the work of those same missionaries had often resulted in mature churches which could deliver the goods. An objective of World Relief was to enable the church to do professional quality relief work.

Encouraging National Christians

Outside specialists and volunteers can be useful in such programs, Ballard thinks, but it works better when national Christians handle them. When recipients of help can identify their helper with a church in their country it also helps the credibility of that church. Using in-country believers is also more economical than sending those from other countries, the long-term director said. He is convinced that all workers must be supervised properly and required to account for funds entrusted to them, but "despite their sin, Christian people are still the most conscientious on earth."

One of his favorite stories of the value of working through the church comes from Burkina Faso, a West African country devastated by drought at the end of the 1980s. One community, sharply divided between Muslim and Christian adherents, was very short on resources. World Relief supplied an emergency grain bank to the church and provided technical help in drilling a well. The evangelicals then gave food and water to the most needy, regardless of religious affiliation.

After the children of one Muslim elder were helped, he conceded to a Christian leader that their unselfishness was so impressive that he wanted his offspring to be Christians. The pastor in that community, Ballard said, "is having a marvelous harvest" and because of the sincere and thorough-going testimony of his people, the converts are not "rice" Christians (who have come only for the material aid).

After initial disappointment upon reading an article about relief work in strife-torn Sri Lanka, the World Relief chief had to admit being pleased that it did not name his agency as the largest donor. Instead, after identifying two other agencies the main thrust of the story was that recipients were "really thankful for what the church was doing for them," he recalled. "That's the way it ought to be," the man who ran an advertising agency before going to World Relief explained.

153

The First Real Experiment

The pattern for working through national churches was established during his "first real experiment," Ballard said. That was in the Philippines, where he worked out an agreement with "Jun" Vencer of that nation's council of evangelical churches to channel contributions through his organization. Ballard and Vencer later led in forming an international relief and development network under the World Evangelical Fellowship.

Other kinds of partnerships were also established to meet special needs. In 1980-81 the subsistence farmers of Cambodia's "bread basket" province, Battambang, were in urgent need of help to survive the ravages of war. Christian and Missionary Alliance personnel who had worked in that field asked for help, and a consortium was set up including the Tear Fund of the United Kingdom, the Salvation Army and others, along with World Relief. More than $7 million was raised. Among the facets of the program was veterinary care of oxen.

"The farmers brought their rickety wagons with sick oxen," Ballad recalled. The animals were vaccinated and the carts were repaired. Farmers were given seed rice and new hoe heads. After the first few recipients went home, the word spread. Farmers then came "from all over the province" to get the help, according to Ballard. They produced a crop that year, and the country was spared a famine.

154

'Relief Cowboys'

One observer of that effort dubbed the young men who World Relief brought in to assist as "relief cowboys." In actuality, they were what the evangelical community knows as MKs—"missionary kids," or the children of missionary parents. Some 80 percent of the front-line staff members were MKs, Ballard indicated, "young and lean and mean" workers who had grown up in the region and who knew the language and culture. He noted the agency was "one up on the Peace Corps" when it had the services of such qualified and motivated young people.

Successful completion of the overseas projects has helped the evangelical community, and particularly NAE, gain credibility in the face of criticism that they cared for souls but not bodies, Ballard believes.

One of the most visible of the World Relief programs climaxed in his last year at the helm. A trickle of Soviet evangelical emigrants turned into a torrent a year after most of Eastern Europe renounced communism. Many of the believers during the glasnost era were encouraged by the changes, but they were convinced that conditions would take a turn for the worst before getting better. Some wanted to leave for Israel and some for Western Europe, but most wanted to go to the United States. When the U.S. government changed its Soviet immigration procedures in 1989, many were caught in a bureaucratic tangle. In order to gain Soviet exit permits, they had, in effect, given up all claim to citizenship and livelihood. Still, they were without entry papers for the U.S.

World Relief, with help from top NAE officials, waged a high-profile campaign to tell Americans about the plight of the refugees (who still feared persecution because of their faith). The administration finally ordered a special waiver for the group, and after processing in Moscow, thousands of them arrived in late 1990. World Relief chartered two jumbo jets to dramatize their departure (as well as the need for resettlement sponsors). Serge Duss, who was then in charge of the Soviet refugee project, flew to Chicago on one of those planes. For him, it was a "very, very emotional experience" that was unforgettable. The usually undemonstrative Russian evangelicals, upon hearing the captain's announcement that they had just left Soviet airspace, broke out in applause and cheers.

16

A Capital Reputation

WITH TONGUE IN CHEEK, one harried member of the NAE Washington staff once told a friend requesting quick service that urgent matters could usually be handled in a day, but the miraculous took a little longer.

One of the association's strengths as it reaches the half century mark is its longevity and the continuity of its leadership. A limited staff has performed extraordinary service for a broad constituency, sometimes very expeditiously. It has taken longer to see results on other matters.

Clyde Taylor did not expect to see instant results when he began a Washington seminar for students. At first it was for a select group from the evangelical citadel, Wheaton College, but then it was expanded to include young people from other Christian colleges who were interested in government. The idea was to expose the students to the concept of putting their faith to work in their vocations, with emphasis on the possibility of serving in the political realm. (The idea caught on in Taylor's own family, where his son went to work for the State Department and is today a senior foreign service officer.)

Public Affairs, Public Witness

Alumni of those seminars are scattered around the world today. Not all work for the government. Some do, and some are in responsible positions in Washington. One who came from Wheaton in 1965, Dan Coats, is now a U.S. senator.

"It was this week in Washington that first introduced me to the 'real' world of Washington," he recalled twenty-six years later. "The people I met and the events I experienced changed my view of Washington from a mysterious, unapproachable place of high politics to a place of real people dealing with understandable issues and open to the questions of an interested, but naive young Wheaton student."

Coats, the first Wheaton alumnus to become a member of Congress, did not return to the nation's capital immediately upon graduation from college. He learned the political ropes in Indiana and did his precinct and county duties "in the trenches." His first Capitol Hill work was as an aide to Dan Quayle, then a member of the House of Representatives. When Quayle moved up to the Senate, Coats ran for the House seat and won it. When Quayle became vice-president, Coats moved up to the Senate. Today he is one of NAE's best friends in Washington.

The capital city is full of organizations advocating a multitude of causes. Some of them are very ad hoc in nature and very temporary. Some appear on the scene with great fanfare but disappear almost as quickly.

"The NAE [Washington office] has been here since 1943 and will be here in 1993 and will be here in 2003," Robert Dugan insisted. He has been director of the Office of Public Affairs since 1978.

Dugan himself traces some of his interest in government back to an NAE event in the nation's capital. In addition to the Federal Seminar for students, Taylor inaugurated a Washington conference (now called the Washington Insight Briefing) for pastors and other church leaders. Dugan attended one of them more than a quarter century ago. As a Conservative Baptist pastor he began attending the association's conventions and then was elected to the board of administration and the executive committee. He resigned from a suburban Denver Conservative Baptist pastorate in 1975 to run (unsuccessfully) for Congress in 1976.

Taylor's seminars for students and church leaders are only two of many long-term programs still paying off years later. It took ten years after he went to Washington to get the first NAE delegation received in the Oval Office, but since then many more have gone, with increasing frequency. Good relations have been built up with many agencies.

From 'One Hat' to a Full Staff

The Office of Public Affairs was never Taylor's full time responsibility. It was only one of the "hats" he wore. During his more than thirty years in Washington he also spent a major part of his time and energy as the chief executive of the Evangelical Foreign Missions Association. The board of NAE also gave him the "general director" reigns for the last decade of his service before retirement in 1974. From time to time he was also the acting chief of the chaplaincy commission and a key official of the World Evangelical Fellowship. For a time he also supervised the operation of a travel service and a purchasing office (under the EFMA umbrella).

"He never seemed to have a problem juggling NAE and EFMA" assignments, Avery Kendall, his assistant for many years recalled.

Taylor might not have had difficulty doing many jobs, but NAE had a major task on its hands filling those roles when he retired. The board laid aside the "general director" post, but it beefed up the job description of Billy Melvin as executive director when Taylor retired in 1974. The versatile Floyd Robertson, who had already taken his first NAE "retirement" as director of the chaplaincy commission, was asked to take the public affairs post in the interim. Wade Coggins, who had assisted Taylor in EFMA, became the director of that agency.

Melvin brought Dugan to Washington in 1978 with a mandate to raise the profile and influence of the Washington office.

"Bob Dugan is doing things that Clyde Taylor dreamed of doing," Miss Kendall declared. "He would be thrilled to see the things that Bob is doing in the area of government affairs."

Growth in NAE itself (now representing forty-eight denominations in addition to its many congregational and individual members) and in NAE's commitment to a Washington voice has made the additional work possible. When Dugan came to work the entire Washington staff (including EFMA and chaplaincy personnel) numbered five. Not counting the EFMA and chaplaincy staffs, who still share space in the Washington office, the public affairs director now has five aides in addition to secretarial-clerical assistants.

Keeping Evangelicals Informed

One way he has tried to widen NAE's influence on national affairs is through *NAE Washington Insight,* a monthly newsletter. One edition is mailed directly to subscribers across the country. Another is sent in batches to churches for insertion in their Sunday bulletins or congregational mailings. While he has been gratified at reports that some government officials and church leaders read it with care, Dugan has been disappointed that more Americans do not subscribe. At one point he expected it to have a circulation of at least a million. The list of individual subscribers is about twelve thousand and the church edition numbers about two-hundred thousand.

The public affairs director saw the newsletter as an essential element in establishing a network of evangelicals who would take their citizenship responsibilities seriously and contact their legislators when prompted by reports in the periodical. It has worked in at least some matters. Dugan said he was told by Sen. Claiborne Pell's office that the mail generated by *Insight* made the difference in passing a tough law on drunk driving.

It may be harder to use such a vehicle to fight more complex legislation. After the "Grove City Bill"* passed—over the president's veto—the NAE office was pelted with questions about why evangelicals didn't know about it or why they didn't have more of an effect on the legislative process. Dugan pointed to numerous newsletter articles over many months spelling out the provisions in the bill and warning against its passage. He did not, however, resort to some of the tactics of other Christian leaders whose

---

* The Grove City Bill was Congress's *reversal* of the Supreme Court's ruling that exempted Grove City College (which did not accept any direct federal funds) from having to comply with all federal anti-discrimination regulations.

followers tied up Capitol Hill switchboards at the last minute with inaccurate information about the legislation. He is convinced that the veto might have been sustained had not members of Congress reacted so strongly against those tactics.

The Role of Resolutions

Christians working in the public policy arena have three options on any political issue, according to Dugan. They are to win, to lose, and to win while losing your testimony. He has chosen to avoid the last one. Some of the groups which came to the capital after he did and which are already gone appeared to be willing to claim some short-term victories at the cost of their integrity.

In addition to ethical considerations, the Washington office's activities are governed by NAE policies. The director is not free to testify in favor of any bill *he* likes or to file a "friend of the court" brief on just any interesting Supreme Court case. Actions of the office are based on existing resolutions of the NAE conventions. In cases of doubt, when a principle enunciated in one of the resolutions is not clearly addressed by the matter in question, the NAE executive committee is asked to decide whether the office should take a position.

"It's clumsy," commented John H. White, president of NAE at one of the times of its highest visibility in the nation's capital (1988-90). "It makes it appear we are not relevant." Nevertheless, the

Geneva College official is convinced there is strength in the procedure of working from established policy. He is a former chairman of the convention resolutions committee and also a former convention coordinator (in 1983, when Ronald Reagan made his famous "evil empire" speech).

The Process of Representation

Throughout NAE's history, the passage of a resolution has been a multistage event including much consultation and with little opportunity for precipitate action. Consensus, not a simple majority vote, has been the goal of the leadership. Any member may propose a topic, but it must be processed through a resolutions committee, then the executive committee, and finally the board of administration before it reaches the convention floor.

That process, White observed, helps assure that pronouncements are not "disconnected from the pew."

Dugan agrees. Though the process is slow, he believes that having the largest possible body of NAE take the ultimate positions gives him a stronger foundation from which to speak. Unlike the spokesmen for some religious groups, the public affairs director can tell a congressional committee that the position he is advocating is not that of just an executive committee of ten or twelve or of a board of one hundred. He may also mention that it sometimes take five or more years for a resolution to "incubate" within the association.

NAE and its Washington office have been involved in more than tracking legislation. Billy Melvin, the executive director, has, for instance, chaired a national coalition monitoring television programming and attempting to persuade the producers and commercial sponsors to eliminate indecency. While Christian Leaders for Responsible Television (known as "CLeaR-TV") has no organic connection to NAE, Melvin's leadership has brought attention to the association.

NAE interest in the overall question of broadcasting standards brought the Federal Communications Commission under the scrutiny of the Washington office. In the era of deregulation, the FCC had been ambivalent about enforcement of standards. The Washington staff raised the question anew as commission vacancies occurred. By law, the last seat to be filled (in 1989) was one reserved for a person affiliated with a party other than the sitting president's. Through White House contacts, the NAE Washington staff suggested Ervin Duggan, who not only met that legal requirement but who also was committed to decency on the airwaves. He was appointed and confirmed. Soon, the commission acted to restrict the hours during which some types of objectionable programming could be broadcast.

Broadcasting in general was a brawling youngster when NAE was started, and television was unknown but to a tiny percentage of Americans. Efforts of the association's leaders to be "salt and light" in

165

this area demonstrate NAE's acceptance of new challenges in a changing society.

Some skirmishes on the national scene are won and some are lost. In all of Clyde Taylor's years as "Mr. Evangelical" in Washington, Dugan pointed out, appointment of a U.S. ambassador to the Vatican was blocked. Yet it was Ronald Reagan, the president who readily opened doors for evangelicals, who appointed the first ambassador to the papal state and had him confirmed.

It is a much more pluralistic nation now than it was in 1942. The congressional agenda "didn't challenge our values" as much then as it does now, the public affairs director observed. Nor were there as many challenges to religious liberty.

When the association first set up shop in the Capital City, it was one of very few offices representing religious bodies. Increasing pluralism, heightened interest in national affairs, and the desire of more single issue groups to have their say are seen in the dozens of such offices now operating.

Cults of all kinds as well as orthodox denominations now have their representatives in Washington. Not only do they speak at the seat of government but also at other points of influence across the land.

So, too, does NAE seek to have an impact at the pressure points. Believing now, as it did in 1942, that it represents historic Christianity, the association continues to be a voice for the unvoiced multitudes.

Appendix A

NAE LEADERSHIP THROUGH THE YEARS

Presidents
Harold J. Ockenga (Presbyterian, USA), 1942-44
Leslie R. Marston (Free Methodist), 1944-46
Rutherford L. Decker (Southern Baptist), 1946-48
Stephen W. Paine (Wesleyan Methodist), 1948-50
Frederick C. Fowler (Presbyterian, USA), 1950-52
Paul S. Rees (Evangelical Covenant), 1952-54
Henry H. Savage (Conservative Baptist), 1954-56
Paul P. Petticord (Evangelical United Brethren), 1956-58
Herbert S. Mekeel (Presbyterian, USA), 1958-60
Thomas F. Zimmerman (Assemblies of God), 1960-62
Robert A. Cook (Evangelical Free), 1962-64
Jared F. Gerig (Missionary Church Association), 1964-66
Rufus Jones (Conservative Baptist), 1966-68
Arnold Olson (Evangelical Free), 1968-70
Hudson T. Armerding (Independent Congregational), 1970-72
Myron F. Boyd (Free Methodist), 1972-74
Paul E. Toms (Conservative Congregational), 1974-76
Nathan Bailey (Christian and Missionary Alliance), 1976-78
Carl H. Lundquist (Baptist General Conference), 1978-80
J. Floyd Williams (Pentecostal Holiness), 1980-82
Arthur E. Gay, Jr. (Conservative Congregational), 1982-84
Robert W. McIntyre (Wesleyan), 1984-86
Ray H. Hughes (Church of God, Cleveland), 1986-88
John H. White (Reformed Presbyterian), 1988-90
B. Edgar Johnson (Nazarene), 1990-92

Staff Directors
J. Elwin Wright (Congregational)
Promotional Director, 1942-43
Field Secretary, 1943-45
Executive Secretary, 1945-47

167

Rutherford L. Decker (Southern Baptist)
Executive Secretary, 1948-1950
Executive Director, 1951-53

George L. Ford (Free Methodist)
Associate Executive Director, 1954-56
Executive Director, 1956-1963
General Director, 1963-64

Clyde W. Taylor (Southern Baptist)
General Director, 1964-74

Arthur M. Climenhaga (Brethren in Christ)
Executive Director, 1964-1967

Billy A. Melvin (Free Will Baptist)
Executive Director, 1967-

Appendix B

NATIONAL ASSOCIATION OF EVANGELICALS MEMBER DENOMINATIONS

Year indicates when denomination joined NAE

Free church tradition

Baptist General Conference (1966)
Brethren Church (1968)
Brethren in Christ Church (1949)
Conservative Baptist Association of America (1990)
Evangelical Free Church of America (1943)
Evangelical Mennonite Church (1944)
Fellowship of Evangelical Bible Churches (1948)
General Association of General Baptists (1988)
National Association of Free Will Baptists* (1946-72)
    Oklahoma State Association of Free Will Baptists (1973)
Mennonite Brethren Churches, U.S. Conference (1946)

Holiness tradition

Christian and Missionary Alliance (1966)
Church of the Nazarene (1984)
Church of United Brethren in Christ (1953)
Churches of Christ in Christian Union (1945)
Evangelical Christian Church (1988)
Evangelical Church of North America (1969)
Evangelical Congregational Church (1962)
Evangelical Friends International, North America (1971)
Evangelical Methodist Church (1952)
Free Methodist Church of North America (1944)

Missionary Church (1944)
Primitive Methodist Church (1946)
Salvation Army (1990)
Wesleyan Church (1948)

Pentecostal tradition

Assemblies of God (1943)
Christian Church of North America (1953)
Church of God, Cleveland (1944)
Church of God of the Mountain Assembly (1981)
Congregational Holiness Church (1990)
Evangelistic Missionary Fellowship (1982)
Elim Fellowship (1947)
Fire Baptized Holiness Church of God of the Americas (1978)
International Church of the Foursquare Gospel (1952)
International Pentecostal Church of Christ (1946)
International Pentecostal Holiness Church (1943)
Open Bible Standard Churches (1943)
Pentecostal Church of God (1954)
Pentecostal Free Will Baptist Church (1988)

Reformed tradition

Christian Reformed Church in North America (1943-51; 1988)
Conservative Congregational Christian Conference (1951)
Evangelical Presbyterian Church (1982)
Midwest Congregational Christian Fellowship (1964)
Presbyterian Church in America (1986)
Reformed Church in America*
    Classis Cascades (1986)
    Synod of Mid-America (1989)
Reformed Episcopal Church (1990)
Reformed Presbyterian Church of North America (1946)

Other traditions
    Advent Christian Church (1986)
    Christian Catholic Church (1975)
    Christian Union (1954)
    World Confessional Lutheran Association (1984)

*Denomination is not currently an NAE member, however, its judicatories listed below are.

Appendix C

U.S. MEMBERSHIP OF NAE DENOMINATIONS
Based upon reports submitted to NAE during 1990

Denomination	Statistical year	Churches	Ordained Ministers	Communicant Members**
Advent Christian Church	89	348	473	18,332
Assemblies of God	89	11,192	17,874	1,266,982
Baptist General Conference	89	789	NR	135,125
Brethren Church	89	126	180	13,155
Brethren in Christ Church	89	187	331	16,842
Christian Catholic Church	89	6	11	*2,000
Christian Church of North America	90	107	246	*13,900
Christian and Missionary Alliance	89	1,829	2,331	134,336
Christian Reformed Church in North America	89	712	1,155	145,308
Christian Union	89	108	179	5,579
Church of God, Cleveland	89	5,580	6,533	509,254
Church of God of the Mountain Assembly	89	103	272	*6,272
Church of the Nazarene	89	5,158	9,061	561,253
Church of the United Brethren in Christ	89	252	300	25,460
Churches of Christ in Christian Union	89	241	600	9,674
Congregational Holiness Church	89	175	333	*7,533
Conservative Baptist Association of America	89	1,124	NR	*204,000
Conservative Congregational Christian Conference	89	180	467	28,413
Elim Fellowship	89	179	318	*20,000
Evangelical Christian Church	89	30	41	1,292
Evangelical Church of North America	89	150	229	12,559
Evangelical Congregational Church	89	158	166	24,772
Evangelical Free Church of America	90	1,044	1,795	106,545
Evangelical Friends International, North American Region	89	238	287	24,955

172

Denomination				
Evangelical Mennonite Church	89	26	52	3,972
Evangelical Methodist Church	89	128	286	8,933
Evangelical Presbyterian Church	90	142	260	42,040
Evangelistic Missionary Fellowship	89	20	71	*1,600
Fellowship of Evangelical Bible Churches	89	18	50	1,942
Fire Baptized Holiness Church of God of the Americas	89	349	825	23,327
Free Methodist Church	89	1,091	1,790	75,871
General Association of General Baptists	89	872	1,245	73,738
International Church of the Foursquare Gospel	89	1,404	3,144	201,025
International Pentecostal Church of Christ	89	92	123	2,914
International Pentecostal Holiness Church	89	1,486	2,095	120,289
Mennonite Brethren Churches, U.S. Conference	89	125	180	16,880
Midwest Congregational Christian Fellowship	89	30	34	*1,500
Missionary Church	89	292	523	26,881
National Association Free Will Baptists#				
Oklahoma State Association	89	261	414	23,915
Open Bible Standard Churches	89	325	944	*40,000
Pentecostal Church of God	88	1,157	1,574	41,699
Pentecostal Free Will Baptist Church	89	141	228	11,985
Presbyterian Church in America	89	1,100	1,950	173,946
Primitive Methodist Church	89	81	101	8,181
Reformed Church In America#				
Classis Cascades	88	13	38	2,488
Synod of Mid-America	89	111	165	26,204
Reformed Episcopal Church	89	83	137	6,019
Reformed Presbyterian Church of North America	89	69	130	3,803
Salvation Army	89	1,122	5,212	115,080
Wesleyan Church	89	1,650	3,076	110,027
World Confessional Lutheran Association	87	12	27	1,182
TOTALS		42,216	67,856	4,458,982

*Estimate
**Represents in most cases baptized adults and young people who have been received into full fellowship—into the communion—of a given congregation. Category is inclusive of ordained ministers but not the children of communicant members.
#Denomination is not currently an NAE member, although its judicatories listed below are.
NR = Not reported

Appendix D

FIFTEEN LARGEST NAE DENOMINATIONS
1989 communicant membership figures

Assemblies of God	1,266,982
Church of the Nazarene	561,253
Church of God, Cleveland	509,254
Conservative Baptist Association of America	204,000
International Church of the Foursquare Gospel	201,025
Presbyterian Church in America	173,946
Christian Reformed Church in North America	145,308
Baptist General Conference	135,125
Christian and Missionary Alliance	134,336
International Pentecostal Holiness Church	120,289
Salvation Army	115,080
Wesleyan Church	110,027
Evangelical Free Church of America	106,545
Free Methodist Church	75,871
General Association of General Baptists	73,738
TOTAL	**3,932,779**

These fifteen denominations represent 88 percent of the combined communicant memberships of all NAE denominations, as shown in Appendix C.

Appendix E

NAE MEMBERSHIP
BY DENOMINATIONAL FAMILIES

Denominational families	1989 membership	Percent
Free church tradition	596,114	13.4%
Holiness tradition	1,139,274	25.6%
Pentecostal tradition	2,266,780	50.8%
Reformed tradition	429,721	9.6%
Other traditions	27,093	0.6%
TOTAL	**4,458,982**	**100.0%**

Selected Bibliography

Cizik, Richard, ed. *The High Cost of Indifference*. Ventura, California: Regal Books, 1984.

Dugan, Robert P., Jr. *Winning the New Civil War*. Portland, Oregon: Multnomah Press, 1991.

Evans, Elizabeth. *The Wright Vision*. Lanham, Maryland: University Press of America, 1991.

Henry, Carl F. H. *Confessions of a Theologian*. Waco, Texas: Word Books, 1986.

Hertzke, Allen D. *Representing God in Washington: The Role of Religious Lobbies in the American Polity*. Knoxville, Tennessee: University of Tennessee Press, 1988.

Howard, David M. *The Dream That Would Not Die: The Birth and Growth of the World Evangelical Fellowship, 1846-1986*. Exeter: Paternoster Press, 1986.

Hunter, James Davison. *Evangelicalism: The Coming Generation*. Chicago: The University of Chicago Press, 1987.

Hutcheson, Richard G., Jr. *God in the White House*. New York: Macmillan Publishing Co., 1988.

Johnston, Arthur. *The Battle for World Evangelism*. Wheaton, Illinois: Tyndale House Publishers, 1978.

Lemcio, Miriam Paine. *Deo Volente: A Biography of Stephen W. Paine*. Houghton, New York: Houghton College Press, 1987.

Lindsell, Harold. *The Battle for the Bible*. Grand Rapids, Michigan: Zondervan Publishing House, 1976.

_____. *The Bible in the Balance*. Grand Rapids, Michigan: Zondervan Publishing House, 1979.

_____. *Park Street Prophet: The Story of Harold Ockenga*. Wheaton, Illinois: Van Kampen Press, 1951.

Murch, James DeForst. *Co-operation Without Compromise: A History of the National Association of Evangelicals*. Grand Rapids, Michigan: Wm. B. Eerdmans Publishing Co., 1956.

NAE Executive Committee, ed. *Evangelical Action! A Report of the Organization of the National Association of Evangelicals for United Action*. Boston: United Action Press, 1942.

Shelley, Bruce. *Evangelicalism in America*. Grand Rapids, Michigan: Wm. B. Eerdmans Publishing Co., 1967.

Index

179

184